Praise for *Let It Rise*

Some authors and teachers are well-informed, diligent students and, therefore, can dispense good information. Then there are those who have actually fleshed out the teaching, put their theories to the test until they are proven, and are now laced with wisdom. These are the leaders who can say with genuine authority, "Here's what works." Mary Jo has mixed the ingredients, kneaded the dough, seasoned it with experience, and baked the bread. You can trust her.

Dutch Sheets
Dutch Sheets Ministries
Author of *Intercessory Prayer*

"You're the Chief Prayer Warrior," I told Mary Jo many years ago when I had the privilege of working with her. Mary Jo's spiritual and organizational calling was clear to me, and this book derives from that calling. She has shown hundreds of people how to pray, how to prepare for and value the Sabbath, and how to yearn for being in the presence of God. Enjoy this book from one of my favorite people and one of the most credible voices on the topic.

Todd Lane
Executive Senior Pastor, Gateway Church

When my friend Mary Jo Pierce decides to talk or write about prayer, she has my full attention. Time and personal experience have taught me that I will always find new insights and fresh wisdom flowing from her lips or her keyboard. This book is no exception. Here, her love of baking and her decades as a leader in the global prayer revival movement mix to form a lovely journey into higher levels of partnership and friendship with our amazing heavenly Father. In each of these 40 brief-but-rich chapters, you'll encounter practical, powerful, and accessible light for moving heaven and earth while drawing ever nearer to Him who is the Bread of Life. His sweet fragrance rises from every page.

David Holland
Author and Teacher
Founding Pastor, The Cup & Table Co.

Mary Jo Pierce is a modern-day Mary of Bethany. Her lifestyle and her writings serve as a compass for stepping beyond the veil of religious busyness and freely sitting at the feet of Jesus. *Let It Rise* welcomes us into Mary Jo's prayer room and kitchen, revealing secrets for cultivating, cooperating with, and carrying God's presence in every season and situation. As one who's been entrusted with building a people of prayer, I find *Let It Rise* to be a treasured resource.

Melissa Medina, MPA
Pastor of Prayer, Trinity Church
Cofounder, HopeFires International
Author of *Praying From Fire: Releasing the Supernatural Through a Life of Prayer*

Mary Jo Pierce has done it once again! Through wit and wisdom, insight and ingenuity, Mary Jo has crafted a masterful work that reflects the Master's crafting of her life of prayer while inviting you into the same work. Pull up a chair and allow Mary Jo to have this fun yet deep conversation with you. Your prayer life will never be the same. Let it rise!

Thomas Miller
Executive Global Strategies Pastor, Gateway Church

Mary Jo's insights on life, love, and nurturing a relationship with God are seasoned with decades of discipline. The modern way she writes about having a relationship with God depicts her very realistic grasp on the diverse challenges we all face today. I love the practical, approachable insights I gained from this book, and I am convinced you will too!

Allan Kelsey
Chief Development Officer, Avodah

We want our lives to be a fragrant aroma to the Lord, but sometimes we get in a rut in our relationship with Him. We grow stagnant. We need a fresh touch. This book will challenge and encourage you to press in without striving, to rest without buying into the world's view of rest, and to resist being satisfied in the outer courts. You will find yourself with new ideas of how to make your life a fragrant aroma to your Lord.

Terri Brown
Co-Pastor, The Table Church in Colorado Springs
Prayer Leader and Author
Terribrown.live

Let it Rise is a living illustration of how the presence of God shows up in the common, painful, or joyful places of life when we pause to pray. The Lord offers healing, second chances, and holy moments that change us forever. We are inspired by Mary Jo's life calling to prayer—it both challenges and nourishes us. Thank you, Mary Jo, for the inspiring nudge to "cultivate, communicate, and carry the presence of God" in every place.

Dr. Wayne D. Wilks, Jr.
Church and Jewish Relations Executive Pastor, Gateway Church
Bonnie Saul Wilks
Author of *Sabbath: A Gift of Time*

Reading through the pages of *Let it Rise*, I am reminded of how much God can do with our "yes." Consistently and faithfully, Mary Jo has devoted her life to cultivating and carrying the presence of God in prayer, worship, warfare, and rest. The joy of baking bread has taken on a life of its own and become one of her greatest sources of revelation of God's enduring love and all-encompassing presence. Every page of this book will build your faith, help you go deeper in your prayer life, and transform your walk with Christ.

Blynda Lane
Trinity Broadcasting Network Spokesperson
Co-host of TBN's *Centerpoint*

Let It Rise is a collection of timely ingredients carefully kneaded together to help shape our lives around the Bread of Life. The aroma of this book will deepen your prayer life.

Matt Knisely
Bestselling Author of *Framing Faith*

Momma Mary Jo, as we affectionately call her, has been a prayer-strength to us for many years. We are thrilled she has invited the reader into her kitchen and prayer room where she has learned to walk so closely with Jesus, the Bread of Life. Her life of prayer is a sweet aroma. And yours will be too!

Will & Dehavilland Ford
Founders of 818 The Sign
www.818thesign.org

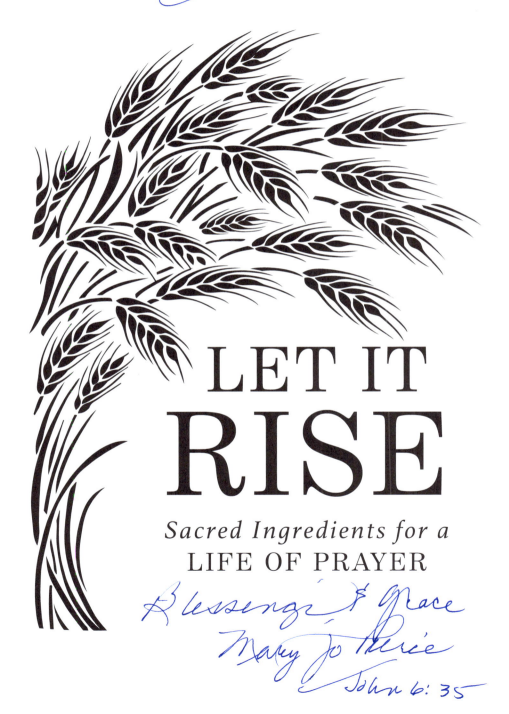

MARY JO PIERCE
Foreword by Mark Harris

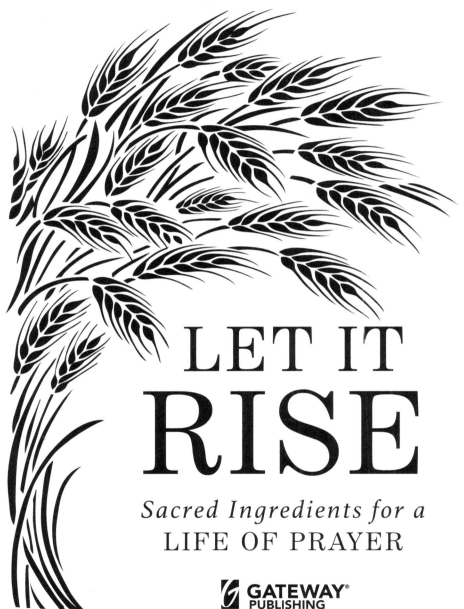

LET IT RISE

Sacred Ingredients for a
LIFE OF PRAYER

GATEWAY®
PUBLISHING

Let It Rise: Sacred Ingredients for a Life of Prayer

Copyright © 2023 by Mary Jo Pierce

Unless otherwise noted, Scripture quotations are taken from the New King James Version®. Copyright © 1982 by Thomas Nelson. Used by permission. All rights reserved.

Scripture quotations marked (AMP) are taken from the Amplified® Bible (AMP), copyright © 2015 by The Lockman Foundation. Used by permission. www.lockman.org.

Scripture quotations marked (ESV) are taken from the ESV® Bible (The Holy Bible, English Standard Version®), copyright © 2001 by Crossway, a publishing ministry of Good News Publishers. Used by permission. All rights reserved. The ESV text may not be quoted in any publication made available to the public by a Creative Commons license. The ESV may not be translated into any other language.

Scripture quotations marked (KJV) are taken from the King James Version. Public domain.

Scripture quotations marked (MSG) are taken from The Message, copyright © 1993, 2002, 2018 by Eugene H. Peterson. Used by permission of NavPress. All rights reserved. Represented by Tyndale House Publishers.

Scripture quotations marked (NIV) are taken from the Holy Bible, New International Version®, NIV®. Copyright © 1973, 1978, 1984, 2011 by Biblica, Inc.™ Used by permission of Zondervan. All rights reserved worldwide. www.zondervan.com. The "NIV" and "New International Version" are trademarks registered in the United States Patent and Trademark Office by Biblica, Inc.™

Scripture quotations marked (NLT) are taken from the Holy Bible, New Living Translation, copyright © 1996, 2004, 2015 by Tyndale House Foundation. Used by permission of Tyndale House Publishers, Carol Stream, Illinois 60188. All rights reserved.

Scripture quotations marked (VOICE) are taken from The Voice™. Copyright © 2012 by Ecclesia Bible Society. Used by permission. All rights reserved.

All rights reserved. No portion of this publication may be reproduced, stored in a retrieval system, or transmitted in any form by any means—electronic, mechanical, photocopying, recording, or any other—without prior permission from the publisher. "Gateway Publishing" and "Gateway Press" are trademarks registered in the United States Patent and Trademark Office by Gateway Church.

ISBN: 978-1-956943-27-6 Paperback
ISBN: 978-1-956943-28-3 eBook

We hope you hear from the Holy Spirit and receive God's richest blessings from this book by Gateway Press. Our purpose is to carry out the mission and vision of Gateway Church through print and digital resources to equip leaders, disciple believers, and advance God's kingdom. For more information on other resources from Gateway Publishing® go to GatewayPublishing.com.

Gateway Press, an imprint of Gateway Publishing
700 Blessed Way
Southlake, TX 76092
GatewayPublishing.com

While the author makes every effort to provide accurate URLs for external or third-party Internet websites at the time of printing, neither she nor the publisher assume any responsibility for changes or errors made after publication.

Cover design by Micah Kandros

Printed in the United States of America
23 24 25 26 27—5 4 3 2 1

TABLE OF CONTENTS

Foreword — xiii
Introduction — xvii

1. Cultivating His Presence — 1
2. Little Things — 7
3. Moses Sealed the Deal — 15
4. I've Got a Friend in You — 21
5. Dialogue, Not Monologue — 27
6. What If? — 35
7. Enough Is Enough — 41
8. From Stale to Sanctified — 47
9. Tending Your Fields — 53
10. I Lay Claim to Your Evenings — 59
11. Sabbath: A Checkup — 65
12. A Divine Invitation — 71
13. A Faith-Trip to the Airport — 77
14. Broken — 83
15. Say Yes to Better Flour — 87
16. Sanctified No — 95
17. Sabbath: A Calling — 99
18. Desperate Times Call for Desperate Praying — 105
19. All-Access Keys — 111

20. Challah-Lujah Hallelujah	115
21. Sabbath: A Commandment	123
22. Treasure Hunting	129
23. Trim the Wick	135
24. Just Keep Trimming	139
25. Prisoners of Hope	147
26. Mantled for His Service	155
27. Sabbath: A Culture	161
28. The Lion That Roars	167
29. Blessed By the Bread	173
30. Kicking Against the Goads	177
31. Trust the Wind	183
32. Just Say Yes	187
33. Too Good Not to Give It Away	191
34. Our Life, a Grain Offering	197
35. Sabbath: A Celebration	201
36. Leave It All on the Field	211
37. Above My Pay Grade	217
38. Sabbath: A Charge to Keep	225
39. Well Done, Done Well	231
40. Becoming Bread	235
Appendix	
Mary Jo's Honey Challah	241
Let It Rise Babka	245
Acknowledgments	249
About the Author	253

Jesus
Bread of Life
Bread from Heaven
Living Bread

For the countless eternal ways You've revealed Yourself
to me in the making and breaking of bread,
both spiritually and in the kitchen ...
For Your example of a life of prayer,
as You sought the Father's will and walked empowered
by the Holy Spirit, and for teaching me to do the same ...
For Your life broken and blessed on the cross and
for how You blessed my broken life at the foot of
the cross ...
For our Emmaus Road revelatory walks,
after which You joined me at my communion table
and blessed and broke bread ...

I pray this labor of love is a sweet aroma to You.
I love you,

Mary Jo

FOREWORD

Mary Jo has a little garden in her yard. It's a bounty of fresh vegetables and herbs, and she often cooks with what she has grown. Now, a lot of people don't care for tomato sandwiches—just grilled bread, fresh tomatoes, salt, pepper, and mayo—but the first time Mary Jo made them for me, I must have eaten five! And the bread she bakes from scratch, many times making up her own recipes, is always delicious. My family has been the recipient of her famous "challah porch drops" many times. But as much as I love her food, the joy of knowing Mary Jo is the real treasure.

Time spent with Mary Jo always yields something good. This has been abundantly true in the nine years I've known her, although it feels much longer. She was one of the first people my wife, Jodie, and I met upon coming to Texas, and we immediately loved her sweet, nurturing disposition. It was like meeting an aunt I never knew I had. And when she needed a worship leader to go on a trip she was leading to Israel, she asked me to come. I packed my guitar, and we went to all the holy sites. Since then, our families have been forever linked—Mary Jo and her husband, Bruce, are part of us, and we are part of them.

When they invited us over for dinner for the first time, my two young adult children, Jodie, and I sat around their beautiful table, and Mary Jo prayed over us. Afterward, she and Bruce led us in communion with freshly baked bread. Beyond the physical food, which was incredible, the dinner was a spiritual meal of God's presence. That night remains one of my fondest memories to this day.

My favorite moments with Mary Jo don't end there, though. I've watched her walk the streets of Israel, lead prayer meetings at church, teach classes in her home, and host beautiful dinners. She is truly precious. She carries a burden of prayer for the Church and for so many individual families. She's not afraid to pray bold prayers, and she's much stronger than you think.

I'm especially grateful for the gift of prayer on Mary Jo's life. The way she intercedes for my family and our ministry brings me to tears. There have been so many times when she's called or texted us at just the right time, and I know I'm not the only person who can say this about Mary Jo. She has a way of making you feel like you're her favorite! I've actually seen people debate over who gets to have her on their prayer team. (She likes me best, though!) She's a sweet, bubbly, and creative lady, but I also love that she's got a bit of fire and sass. I think you'll know what I mean as you read this book. You'll also find out that her life is anything but happenstance. There is intentionality in everything she does.

When I served as the campus worship pastor at Gateway Church Southlake, I would invite Mary Jo to the green room before our Easter services to serve communion to our worship team members. She would bring her homemade challah and some juice. So many times, she would get up to pray for the group and then pause. The first time she did it, I thought, *Oh, is she not going to pray?* But then I realized she did it on purpose. She was intentionally listening first to what the Holy Spirit wanted her to say. She places such high value on not only speaking to God but also hearing from Him—so much so that she has a prayer chair *and* a listening chair! Most of what I've learned about listening to God speak and honoring the Sabbath comes from Mary Jo. So often, I have operated with a "ready, fire, aim" mentality. My prayer life was centered around me telling God what I wanted to tell Him, but she's taught me the value of pausing, being quiet, and letting God speak and sing over me.

That's why this book you're holding is so important! As a worship pastor, I can say what's missing in most believers' lives more than anything else is rest. We're caught up in the busyness of life. We're pouring out and not receiving or refilling. We're talking and not listening. But we need to slow down. I know firsthand how unhealthy it is to not pause and honor the Sabbath each week. We can't afford to miss God's presence or rest. Mary Jo is the voice the Church needs right now.

So take a seat and turn the page. You're invited into the presence of God through prayer, baking, Sabbath, rest, worship, grief, and spiritual warfare. Yes, Mary Jo talks about the process of baking bread throughout the book, but if you dig deeper, it's not really about the bread. It's about experiencing the presence of God and allowing the Holy Spirit to speak to you through the seemingly ordinary. It doesn't matter whether you love being in the kitchen or not. It doesn't matter if you're male or female, old or young—God is inviting us *all* to the table to be with Him. No matter what stage of life you're in, I know you will find incredible wisdom to apply to your life within these pages.

Mary Jo has labored over this book. I wish you could see the time, tears, and prayer she put into writing it. And it's all for *you*. She is a gift to the body of Christ, and I know this book will be as well.

Mark Harris
Grammy-Nominated Artist
Worship Pastor, Gateway Church

INTRODUCTION

BEGIN WITH BREAD

> Blessed is he who shall eat bread in the kingdom of God.
> —Luke 14:15

I love to bake bread. I love the ingredients. I love the process. I love the time it takes. I love watching the different stages of fermenting, mixing, kneading, and rising. And then the pièce de résistance: that final sweet aroma that fills my home and my heart. I *love* baking bread.

What in the world does baking bread have to do with a life of prayer? you may wonder. Truth be told, baking bread was simply the vehicle God used to enrich every part of my prayer life. At first, making, serving, and giving away bread was something new that I immensely enjoyed. Then *the conversation* began. You know, the one where God totally interrupts your life and takes you down an answered prayer road you didn't know to pray! What began as a new "hobby" turned into God introducing me to a *breadth* in my relationship and partnership with Him. Like the yeast that activates flour and causes it to rise and taste all kinds of yummy, God used this simple yet enjoyable engagement with a few ingredients to impact and influence every aspect of my life of prayer.

Enriched bread—that's what my life became. Scriptures that had manna, grain, rest, wheat, Shiloh, showbread, dew, or anything and everything related to bread and the presence of God became an allegory in my life. And this is my prayer for you: that God will take our Bread of Life, Jesus, and transform your life into living bread, carrying His presence.

God tied all this together for me with Scriptures that speak to how bread represents His presence. From the showbread in the Tabernacle of Moses to Jesus' own declarations of "I am the bread of life" (John 6:35, 48 NIV). From seeing and applying Scripture (manna) to prayer strategies (partnership) to learning about Sabbath and God's gift of rest. Psalm 23:5—"You prepare a table before me in the presence of my enemies"—brought spiritual warfare to an entirely new battlefield, and my heart swells just writing this!

After almost 50 years of walking closely and intentionally with Jesus, I found the deeper application of "everything bread" to a life of prayer: *our prayer lives center around cultivating, cooperating with, and carrying His presence with us wherever we go.*

This book was written during a global crisis—not just a medical crisis but also wars and rumors of wars and a battle for "One Nation Under God." In the true nature of God who works something good for those who love Him and are called to His purpose (see Romans 8:28), we are experiencing a powerful emerging prayer movement. The world is trying to cancel many things, including our voices, but the Holy Spirit can't and won't be canceled. Our faith *will* be strengthened, and we will find ourselves very Joshua-like—praying bold, courageous, and strong prayers.

There is an increased desire and desperation to know God, hear His voice, and feel His presence in all the shaking going on around us. There is a growing need to develop a thriving, intimate relationship with the Father, Son, and Holy Spirit. The world is looking for answers and for truth. For God to engage powerfully against the forces of evil, we must carry His presence into places, situations, and circumstances we wouldn't have imagined. As we navigate through the Scriptures, we need the deep, abiding presence of God to go with us from our "tent of meeting" (Exodus 33:7) to the mission field.

There are signs of revival all around. If we lean in, we can hear "the sound of marching in the tops of the poplar trees" (2 Samuel 5:24 NIV). We will be prepared! Prayer is our answer—deep, abiding, powerful, living prayer!

The book you are holding was written for men and women, young and old. I mean "young" in the ways of prayer and "old" in the sense of those who have walked closely with the Lord for decades.

Through the chapters we will closely examine our prayer lives and see God at work, transforming us into the joyful houses of prayer (see Isaiah 56:7) so needed from now to eternity. We will look at different aspects and applications of a life of prayer, from stewardship to relationship to ultimate partnership with God. From here to eternity.

In a way, it's a different kind of cookbook. Whether prayer or baking, there are basic ingredients. Then we add inspiration for the unique need or occasion.

We need to connect to God and the active, powerful, two-edged sword of His Word. We need to know His will, walk in His ways, and pray in the power of the Spirit. Family, friends, and strangers desperately want God to engage in their lives; they want help and answers to prayer more than ever before. *There is no problem in one's prayer life that God doesn't have an answer to!*

The prayers of the faithful written in Scripture are symbolized by incense. From Exodus 30 in the Tabernacle, where Aaron's prayer offerings were made on the altar for burning incense, to Revelation 8:4, where "the smoke of the incense, with the prayers of the saints, rose before God." Let it rise!

Let the fragrance of our lives of prayer be poured out like the worship depicted in John 12:3 as Mary anointed Jesus' feet. Let it rise!

As with the aroma of freshly baked bread, let us spread the aroma of the Bread of Life (Jesus) everywhere. May the sacred ingredients of our lives of prayer become salt and light to the hungry and thirsty souls with whom God connects us. Let it rise!

Blessed are you as you partake of the Bread of His presence throughout this book. Blessed shall you be as the Holy Spirit rests on and refreshes you by the Word and ways of God as you learn to live prayer out loud!

Place the bread of the
Presence on the table
and keep it before
Me at all times.

Exodus 25:30 VOICE

1

CULTIVATING HIS PRESENCE

Andrew and Norine Brunson had been missionaries in Istanbul, Turkey, for 23 years when the unimaginable occurred—they were arrested and imprisoned under false charges. News of the Brunsons' arrest made international headlines, but it took on special meaning to me because I knew this couple. I had met them years earlier when I went with a church team to Turkey, and now my prayers joined with thousands of believers throughout the global body of Christ who were beseeching God to right a terrible wrong.

Norine was released after 13 days, but it was not until two years later that Andrew miraculously regained his freedom. He then shared with the watching world an incredible testimony about the power of prayer and the utmost importance of cultivating the presence of God.

For the first 13 days of their incarceration, Andrew and Norine shared a crowded cell filled with other prisoners. What they did not share, however, was the same demeanor. Even with all his degrees, biblical studies, and years as a pastor, Andrew was troubled by fear and dread regarding the unknown charges and unstable political climate. But as he observed Norine, he couldn't help seeing how peaceful his faith-filled wife was. She carried such peace and faith, even in that intimidating prison cell. Andrew concluded that Norine's consistent, daily time with God (versus his sporadic "quiet" times with God) was what made the difference.[1]

What a testimony to cultivating the presence of God in one's life! This story from my friends underscored a long-held belief that *it is the presence of God that keeps us in times of joy and times of despair.*

It reminded me of Moses and the Tent of Meeting (Exodus 33:7–23). This leader knew the cloud-by-day and fire-by-night presence of God. He knew the burning bush presence of God. He knew the bread of His presence (showbread) in the Tabernacle. Yet here in the Tent of Meeting, an intentional place to meet with God pitched outside the busyness of camp, Moses spoke to God face-to-face. And it is there that God called him "friend" and promised to go with him into uncharted territory.

This Tent of Meeting conversation declared Moses's need for God's presence and God's promise to be with him. Beloved readers, this is what we desire and need for the days in which we are living. We want to recognize His voice and understand His ways. The peace of God. The loving care of God. The I-will-never-leave-you-or-forsake-you promise of God.

We know the why. Now let's consider the how! Allow me to suggest a place. A beginning place. A sent-from place. A place where you learn to hear His voice and hide His Word in your heart. A place that strengthens every part of your personal relationship with the Father, Son, and Holy Spirit. A place of

---

1. Andrew Brunson, *God's Hostage* (Grand Rapids, MI: Baker Books, 2019).

surrender and commitment. This is the place when you meet with God for the purpose of developing and nurturing His presence in your life.

For me, this place is my dedicated prayer chair in my prayer room. In this chair, I lay aside my Bible study, reading time, and longer-than-my-arm list of prayer needs, and I focus solely on cultivating His presence.

How is this possible? It certainly isn't easy to lay aside *everything* else, so I sought the Lord on how to do this in a practical manner. He gave me three steps:

1. Be Fully Present

> Be silent in the presence of the Lord God;
> For the day of the Lord *is* at hand,
> For the Lord has prepared a sacrifice;
> He has invited His guests (Zephaniah 1:7).

The Lord whispered, "Be fully present." He wanted 100% of me. Because I am easily distracted, I had to intentionally quiet myself. I had to determine to lay my cares, concerns, and troubles aside to focus on the audience of One. I had to remove distractions that sent me on detours or dead ends and delayed my connecting with God. I was on a personal mission to learn to be fully present. It took time. It took perseverance. It took practice. But it worked. The Holy Spirit built within me a quiet spirit where I was fully present.

2. Be Fully in His Presence

> He said, "My Presence will go *with you,* and I will give you rest" (Exodus 33:14).

The word rest in this verse means "soothes, comforts, and quiets." I noticed when I become and stay still, I sense a peace and a presence. A Person. I am not alone; God is with me. I have drawn near to God, and He is drawing near to me (see James 4:8). The cares of both my inner world and the outer world take on a new perspective in light of being with Him. I find myself meditating on one of His names. Wanting nothing more than to get to know Him! I discovered that abiding place Jesus prayed for us in John 17.

3. Be Fully Satisfied

As for me, I will see Your face in righteousness;
I shall be satisfied when I awake in Your likeness (Psalm 17:15).

I have a conversation with the Lord. A Scripture comes to mind, so I read and pray it. I linger and let God speak. A person or situation comes to my mind, and I ask, "Father, how do You want me to pray?" After a time of prayer, whether minutes or hours later, my spirit senses "Amen." God has filled me up, and I am ready to leave this special time and greet the day. From this dedicated place I will carry His presence wherever I go and to whomever I meet.

The more we cultivate His presence, the more we know and recognize the fullness of God with us wherever we go. Carrying His presence changes the atmosphere!

There is an urgency in my spirit. A deep sensing that God is calling us to develop strong spiritual muscles. A newfound fortitude and stamina for the day at hand and the days ahead. How does one develop such a strength to endure when the unplanned, unprepared, unthinkable happens? The answer is not complicated. It's not difficult. However, as Andrew and Norine discovered, it does take dedication and time!

> Here we are, Lord. Something is stirring deep inside us. We know there is so much more of You—knowing You and living in Your presence. We purpose to seek You with our whole hearts, souls, and minds. We are here, Lord. Wanting. Willing. Waiting. In Jesus' name, Amen.

2

LITTLE THINGS
My Second Prayer Room

"Don't try to understand it. Just respect it." This quote made me laugh! It could easily be referring to the awe and wonder of making challah, the traditional Jewish bread served at the weekly Sabbath meal. This simple act of worship, going back centuries and linking us to generations of families, invites the very presence of God into the process. Who can fathom all He does in us through this simple task of making bread? It's mysterious! It's miraculous! It's wonderful! Don't try to understand it. Just respect it.

Today, I'm inviting you into my kitchen. So much more than a place to prepare meals, it has become my second prayer room. Yes, it's my second special, set-apart place to meet with God. From this place, the Holy Spirit has taught me a whole new way to worship, pray, enjoy, and connect with God. He's taught me a whole new way to practice His presence.

Since my first attempt at making bread, I was captivated by the entire process. I eventually graduated from YouTube University, where I learned a little about the wonder of mixing, waiting, kneading, braiding, resting, and rising. Ultimately the aroma of freshly baked bread became my love offering to the Lord, and in the process my heart and kitchen made a new place for the presence of God!

In the Old Testament, the priests—all men—baked the bread. In fact, I'm almost certain women weren't allowed in the Tabernacle kitchen. Of course, today in Jewish homes, tradition has women making challah bread. However, after having hosted more than 700 men and women in my kitchen, I have received enough testimonies to know that making bread is a *family* affair. Whether throwing pizza dough or braiding bread, it's all hands on deck. The countless pictures and stories I receive from both men and women will attest to this!

I realize that baking isn't everyone's way to connect with God. I recently heard a man give testimony to experiencing God's presence while making surfboards. It was what he was created to do. I encourage you to find your own "God-zone." Fishing, walking, needlework, woodwork .... the list of possibilities is endless.

But for today, we are in my kitchen, sharing the life application lessons God has taught me in the wonder of making challah bread. When He invited me into my kitchen, I discovered new ways to enter His presence. New ways to worship through baking. New ways to share my love of prayer in my apron. I found a new language to bless. And I found new ways to encourage men, women, and children to seek God about rest and Sabbath.

It was so good of God.

So kind.

So Father-like.

So insightful.

With apron donned and recipe in hand, I sing along with Messianic worship leader Marty Goetz, and I worship as I mix, knead, braid, and bake challah. I think of Brother Lawrence, a 17th century monk who delighted in the mundane details of everyday life as he experienced the presence of God in his kitchen. My challah ingredients are lined up and ready to do what they were created to do. I pause and do what I was created to do—pray! I invite God's presence into my kitchen and ask for His blessings on this simple task that will soon become a love offering. After all, on this bread-represents-the-presence-of-God baking day, my kitchen is my second prayer room.

APRON

My apron becomes my "prayer shawl" when I'm baking challah bread. I'm reminded of Susannah Wesley's testimony. Her apron became a tent of meeting, and when she lifted it over her head, her 10 children (including the future theologians John and Charles Wesley) knew that "Momma was praying."

This week I washed my 49 aprons. They are fresh and ready for my Acts 2:42 Challah-Day group coming over next week. I can't wait! I talk about these days throughout this book. They are filled with friends, baking, prayer, and journaling in my home. My kitchen and my heart love having eager, attentive, and all-hands-in-the-flour groups over. Today I glanced into my utility room and beheld my aprons. They were hanging over a chair with waist and neck straps touching the floor. For one holy, stop-and-ponder moment, the apron strings looked like Jewish prayer shawl tallit tassels.

YEAST

As I get lost in the process of activating the yeast (just add a little heat and sweet), I think of Matthew 13:33: "The kingdom of heaven is like yeast" (NIV). And I pray that like each itsy-bitsy speck of yeast, God will use our lives and His Church to permeate the world with His presence and love. I watch the yeast rise and picture how God takes our little and does so much to glorify Him and impact His kingdom. Let it rise!

MIXER

After I add all the ingredients to my mixing bowl, I turn the power on and listen to the hum of my mixer as it swirls a symphony of sacred ingredients. This mixer is my guitar. Bread baking is my act of worship!

KNEADING

I always knead my dough about 100 times and pray for a hundredfold blessing on those who are going to partake of my love offering. (It so happens that this is also the number of times needed to get silky, bouncy dough.) And while I do that, I think of the prayers the Israelites must have prayed as they fled Egypt—"So the people took their dough before it was leavened, their kneading bowls being bound up in their clothes on their shoulders" (Exodus 12:34 AMP).

Imagine my joy when I discovered this gold nugget in Scripture.

> Your basket will be blessed; *it will be full at harvest time,*
> and your kneading bowl *will be blessed; you'll always have
> plenty of bread* (Deuteronomy 28:5 VOICE).

Every time I knead my bread, I am prophetically declaring that these braided loaves will carry a blessing for the recipients and will minister to those sick, hurting, lonely ... whatever their personal need might be. And I agree with the Scripture that at their harvest time, there will be plenty of bread (the presence of God). Amen!

Today, I have a beautiful kneading bowl sitting on my dining table. It's a constant reminder of God's work in my life. He takes the few humble ingredients of our lives, and through the kneading work of the Holy Spirit, He turns us into a love offering!

BRAIDING

Traditional challah bread is a three-strand loaf. This braid looks like arms hugging! It reminds me of Ecclesiastes 4:12:

> Though one may be overpowered,
>   two can defend themselves.
> A cord of three strands is not quickly broken (NIV).

As we come together at the Shabbat meal and lift our loaves of challah as an offering to our Lord, in Him, we are stronger and more united than ever!

REST

The dough has two resting periods. Again, it is a visual of needing rest—body, soul, and spirit—so we can rise and be all we were created to be. Oh, the fun of watching this happen! One of my treasured memories is watching the utter surprise on my granddaughters' faces when they removed the tea towel (see below) from the bowl. Samantha and Cassidy could not believe what had happened to that little ball of dough!

TEA TOWELS

I have a collection of tea towels I use to put over the bread during the resting periods. The towels take on special meaning depending on whom I'm baking and praying for that day. Following an Acts 2:42 Challah-Day, my friend Tiffany went home to find a tea towel her grandmother had hand-stitched. That towel says, "Count your blessings the rest of your life" and has a little family stitched underneath. This is now Tiffany's traditional challah bread towel and family heirloom. It's the little things, like tea towels, that increase the joy of challah bread and all it entails.

CHALLAH

It takes time to make challah bread. That in itself is a gift. The ingredients, the mixing, the kneading, the rising (not once but twice), the braiding, the baking, the smell ... Oh, just writing about it transports me to the joy of taking the time to slow down and experience the process.

When our kitchen turns into a prayer room, and we mix, knead, pray, worship, and reap a harvest of freshly baked bread from our labors ... well, it's just a good, God-plan! I'll leave you with these beautiful words by my friend John Andersen. Just look what God can do with our bread!

> When she made bread for the prophet,
> the widow of Zarephath saved her child's life.
> When she gathered grain for bread,
> Ruth found love.
> When she gave bread to the spies,
> Rahab rescued her whole family.
> When God dropped bread from heaven,
> He fed the nation.
> When Jesus broke bread,
> He showed how He would save the world.
> When He broke bread again at Emmaus,
> the two disciples saw death did not defeat Him.
> And then He broke it one more time by the seashore,
> and He redeemed His broken follower.
> Lord, I need bread.
> Save me.
> Rescue me.
> Redeem me.
> Feed me.

3

MOSES SEALED THE DEAL

Matthew 6:6 instructs us to go into our room, shut the door, and pray to God. That Scripture has always intrigued me. It's an invitation but also a rather strong directive: "This *is* the way, walk in it" (Isaiah 30:21). We all need a designated place. A private place. A sacred place.

For the longest time, I was a nomad, wandering like the Israelites. I travelled from chair to couch, bed to back porch, table to desk. I never really felt settled until I read that Moses's "room" was his tent. And this was not just any tent. This tent was pitched away from the busyness of camp for the specific reason to meet with God. That's what I wanted! A tent of meeting. A place sanctified, set apart, and consecrated to meeting with God.

The beloved Scriptures God gives us in Exodus 33:7–18 perfectly speak to Moses's strategy of removing himself from the busyness of camp and pitching his tent to intentionally meet with God. I often wonder what gave him this idea. Was it his experience on the mountain with the burning bush? Away from the murmuring and complaining and noise of life, God called that place "holy ground." Did that put a hunger and a need in

Moses to replicate that setting to be with God and to hear from God?

I have a favorite word: *tentology*. You won't find it in the dictionary, because I made it up. Simply put, tentology is the study of meeting with God. It encompasses the whole of my life mission. I guess that makes me a tentologist! When I first became a tentologist, I didn't know how much I had to learn. How much God wanted to teach me about meeting with Him. How intentional He was about "pitching a tent" in my life and in my heart to meet with Him.

I love reading various synonyms for "tent" in Scripture:

- Temple
- Tabernacle
- Habitation
- Booth
- Hut
- Dwelling Place.

Each word draws me to a place—my prayer room, my prayer chair, my heart. Each place speaks to a created, cultivated, and cared-for place where God speaks and I listen, and I listen and God speaks.

Over the years I have found this principle hidden everywhere in Scripture. God wants me to be intentional about meeting with Him. He wants to train my ear to hear and my heart to respond. My tent of meeting—no matter where I am physically—is an anchor that keeps me

- learning to sense His presence,
- learning to listen to His whisper, and
- learning to yield my heart.

This book is all about cultivating, communing with, and carrying the presence of God. *And this meeting place is where it starts.* Where it happens. Where God's heaven meets your earth.

My life Scripture hangs in my prayer room:

> As for me, Father, because of Jesus' righteousness and therefore my right standing with you, I will be fully satisfied when I awake in the morning seeing you face to face and having sweet communion with you (Psalm 17:15 MJP).

(MJP stands for "Mary Jo Pierce." You will see my initials whenever I put a verse into my own words.)

Saints, I believe God wants this for us—that we would know His presence in such a face-to-face encounter that we could be fully satisfied. Fully satisfied in knowing that God is engaged with our thoughts, needs, and desires. Fully satisfied and fully accepted in Christ, our Mediator. A place where, like Moses, we can meet with God and hear Him call us "friend." And then, whether or not our prayers are answered at that time, there is a knowing of "I'll go with you and give you rest." God's desire is to meet with you in a sanctified, set-apart, meeting place. Why, even our favorite Peter thought it was a good idea to pitch a tent away from the crowds and enjoy the presence and manifested glory of God when Jesus was on the mountain top with Elijah and Moses (see Luke 9:33)!

I once participated in a six-day equipping seminar. The classes were built around prayer and intercession with an emphasis on prophetic gifts. There were so many exercises on hearing God as we grew in confidence on ways to encourage, comfort, and edify others. However, there was one moment—one word—that preached to me then and still does to this day. The word was *intentional.* (Notice that "tent" is in bold!) I cannot even tell you the context in which the word was delivered, but God was prepared to speak volumes to me about how to live my life in Christ. At that time, I already had my prayer chair and prayer room. This word underscored the value God was placing on it.

After reading my first book, *Adventures in Prayer*, my friend Yvette told me she was challenged to find a place to meet with God. She said, "I don't have a prayer room, but I have a prayer corner. It's in my bedroom, and in the corner, I put a designated, set-apart chair. The first thing I see when I wake up is my prayer corner. I have a wall hanging that says, 'Blessed' in rather large letters. It's a wonderful way to start my day!"

Yvette suggested this space in her bedroom was not the "best" place. I assured her, it's not about the best place; God looks at the intention of the heart! Like my busy, married, mother-of-four friend who lives in a not-enough-space apartment. She needed a place to meet with God. Weeks after we prayed, she was overjoyed! Her face shining, she told me God indeed found a place for her. It happens to be her bathtub where she sits with her Bible and journal—but no water! Can you imagine the glory cloud that rests over her tub when she meets with Him? The purity of the heart, the intentionality of it ... that's what God is looking at!

Recently, I attended a double celebration memorial for the parents of my dear friend Jayme. Mickey and his wife, Judy, lived in a retirement home and were devoted followers of Jesus. Eighty years young, Mickey had read my first book, *Adventures in Prayer,* and was drawn to the idea of a prayer chair. He not only liked the idea, but he also actually picked a chair that became his dedicated place to meet with God. This was where he truly learned the presence of God. Oh, the stories he shared with his family of the miraculous transformations that came from his meeting place. At Mickey's funeral, his granddaughter Emily testified of his prayer chair and how God used it to take a mature follower of Christ and introduce him to a deeper relationship with Him and the Word. It is never too late to start!

When I was on staff at Gateway Church, one of my favorite people, Pastor Todd Lane, was my oversight for a season. He told me his desire was that I felt set, settled, and secure in my calling and ministry. I loved that! That was his desire, my desire, and God's desire. And it reminded me of my prayer chair, where I truly was set, settled, and secure. So I took what God and I did in my prayer chair—all the conversations, prayers, instructions, fasting, and blessings—and carried that into ministry.

Matthew 7:16 says, "You will know them by their fruits." I examined Scripture and read of the cloud of God's presence covering the tent door. I saw God call Moses "friend" and then promise that His presence would go with him and give him rest (see Exodus 33:14). I wish Scripture expounded on the conversations God and Moses had in this set-apart tent. What did God say that emboldened, empowered, and encouraged Moses to continue his assignment to lead these precious, chosen people into their promised land? I wanted that kind of fruit to come from my time with God in my tent-chair. So I took notes from Moses's (and Joshua's) time spent in the tent pitched away from camp. Moses sealed the deal for me. Knowing and hearing God is a must!

Ultimately, our tent of meeting, whether a chair, a corner, or a bathtub, becomes a portable tent within our heart. You can carry God's presence with you wherever you go! And just as God promised Moses, He will go with you and give you rest.

4

I'VE GOT A FRIEND IN YOU

"You're my best friend." These heartfelt words slipped out of my mouth as I sat on my bed with my much-loved Hugging Bible on my lap. The year 2020 was an isolated, fearful time. It was a time of washing groceries, wearing gloves and masks, and sequestering from others. The loneliness was deafening. The pandemic prompted an endless stream of internal and external questions to address everything being shaken around me. I looked at my Bible resting open on my lap, and a sense of "I AM" was with me.

"You're my best friend," I repeated to my Bible, as if it could hear me speak these words. "There is no one who knows me better than you. Not even my husband of 44 years." These pages, wrinkled, torn, tear-stained, underlined, and highlighted, with so many notes in the columns, have walked with me through life in Christ. I have searched for a word, a principle, a character quality, an answer, a prayer, a wilderness, a mountain to go to, a tree to rest under ... and I have found them there, inside my best friend.

After having my Hugging Bible rebound because it was falling apart, I tucked a note inside. I want to share it with you now:

Welcome home, Hugging Bible. All the years of loving you, teaching you, praying you, studying you, crying you, pondering you. Hearing, seeking, and finding through these beloved pages. You needed repair. But only the outside was changed. The inside still holds the same love and friendship, truths, and conversations. The same tear-stained pages, and underlined verses, and highlighted words. My Friend, my Bible.

I don't take having and holding the infallible, Spirit-inspired Word of God for granted. I can't. When I think of what it must be like to not have the Word, my heart sinks. I think of the ministries that are giving themselves to translating and getting the Word to "the uttermost part of the earth" (Acts 1:8 KJV). I think of those in prison without a Bible. I am inspired by the stories of the prisoners of war in Vietnam who would send memorized Scriptures via Morse code to fellow prisoners. I think of those who have not been introduced to the Word, to the manna that walks us into the chapters, verses, and words from thousands of years ago as if they were written for us today.

There are so many translations of Bibles. However, there is a very special, very personal, and very prophetic version not available in any store. That's the Bible where you put your name in place of Gideon, Mary, Paul, Naomi, and so on. It's the one where you find yourself wandering through the wilderness. It's the one where you identify with a desperate Hannah, a denying Peter, or a despondent David. By the way, when you read the Scriptures, you need to know that the principles apply to both men and women. I know lots of Martha-like men and hearts-after-God women!

Years ago, I began mentoring two high school-aged girls. We gathered in my prayer room, sitting cross-legged with our Bibles, journals, and pens. The first question I asked was, "If God never answered a prayer, would you still pray?" Jesus modeled it in "Our Father, who art in heaven" long before He said, "Give us this day our daily bread." The quest to grow in your relationship and partnership with God is predicated on *Who* the Holy Trinity is. As you learn the Who of God—Father, Jesus, and Holy Spirit—you will discover you cannot *not* pray.

Your living prayer will become the natural overflow of learning God's character, will, heart, and desires. You will discover the way He cares for and keeps you, and you will learn to trust in what His plans and purposes are for your life.

Years ago, I was invited by my Michigan pastor, Tim Taylor, to do a weekend prayer conference at Hope Church. I talked about how to pray the names of God, how to identify with the character and heart of God, and how to live with the confidence and authority of Whose we are. We're blood-bought, redeemed, and forgiven sons and daughters with access to the King through prayer!

I wish I could share my entire conference talk with you, but here are two highlights:

1. Give the Word room to breathe.

A spirit of religion will choke the truth of God. It will distort what God wants to say to you. We need to filter the Word of God through what it says about how He sees us and not how we see ourselves (or even how others see us). When we do that, we give the Spirit the liberty, the freedom, and the breath-of-God to speak to us. He will teach us, nurture us, and grow us into houses of prayer that echo His heart, will, plans, and purposes. We will carry the Word we have meditated on, and we will be transformed by it.

2. Be doers, not just hearers, of the Word.

A close friend once paid me the highest compliment by calling me "a steward of the Word of God." He had watched how I had taken the Word of God, both written and spoken, and built my life around it. Treasured it. Sowed it into others' lives. I had to think about that comment and talk to God about it. I do put a great deal of value, importance, and responsibility in what God shows me, teaches me, says to me, and directs me through His Word. How He has me pray it. How He instructs me to be a sower, through both prayer and words of encouragement. I want to steward the seeds of God's truth in people's lives and marriages, in their faith and healings, and in their sorrow and sadness. I think that compliment was the most wonderful thing anybody could say to me.

As you read the Word, there will be Scriptures that convict you, call you to act, or charge you to go. This is the hard part. This is the easy part. This is the rubber-meets-the-road part. This is the adventure part. This is the heaven to earth part. This is the challenging part. This is the living outside your comfort zone part. This is the Spirit is alive and active in me part.

> But prove yourselves doers of the word [actively and continually obeying God's precepts], and not merely listeners [who hear the word but fail to internalize its meaning], deluding yourselves [by unsound reasoning contrary to the truth] (James 1:22 AMP).

Right now, the Holy Spirit is nudging me to tell you, "Timing is key." God will have you marinate, measure, and mark His

Word before you act on it. I've missed God on occasions and spoken or acted too soon. I didn't give God time to go before me to prepare the person, condition, or situation. God is a God of perfect timing, and His Word brings perfect guidance to our lives.

5

DIALOGUE, NOT MONOLOGUE

Stacks of journals line my bookshelf. These journals each have a beauty of their own—three-ringed, leather-bound, fancy fabrics, every imaginable size and shape. Each one-of-a-kind journal has a unique personality with its own strengths and weaknesses. And inside each of these history books is the unfolding story of a relationship and partnership with my God.

The pages in these journals are highlighted, tear-stained, and scripted in longhand, scribble, print, or cursive. Some pages have thoughts written up the sides, and other pages lie empty, waiting for responses or prayers not yet prayed. These journals are like dear old friends who have kept secrets, laughed and cried with me, and believed the best even in the worst of times. Like soldiers reporting for duty, these journals retell the lost battles and victories of days past.

There is no question that my journals are my favorite books. They are all non-fiction! They represent my heart "set on pilgrimage" (Psalm 84:5) and record what God is saying to me. Personal. Up front. Face-to-face. Some blessings. Some correction. Some teaching. Some inspiration. Yes, we can be inspired by our own journals. They are the written records of our relationship and partnership with God—Father, Jesus, and the Holy Spirit.

There's a reason why, when I teach my three living prayer non-negotiables, journaling is number three—right behind a prayer chair designated to meet with God and your Bible. There is a God-reason He directed me to devote a chapter to this topic. It is not my purpose to provide you with the *how* of journaling. There is no wrong way to journal; after all, there are no "journaling rules"! It comes down to the Who and the why. And I suspect God has more reasons to emphasize about this spiritual discipline. Doing it. Mentoring it. Modeling it. When God speaks, it merits recording. We do our part. He'll do His part!

Why do I call this chapter "Dialogue, Not Monologue"? Monologues are diaries, places for you to record events, experiences, and day-to-day details. It's not that these topics cannot be covered in your journals, but what makes a journal different is that you are prompted by the Holy Spirit to ask questions and then examine, review, and rejoice in God's responses.

My friend Pastor Neal Seiwert once viewed journaling as something that just wasn't for him. He thought of it as a diary where all his feelings and emotions would be on paper. What if someone found it? And diaries are not for men!

But something changed in Neal's heart and mind, and he shared the following with me:

> Now I know that wrong thinking cost me precious time writing down Scriptures that spoke to me, revelation God was giving to me, and deep things in my heart that needed to *get out*.
>
> To me, having a pen in hand and paper ready points to an expectation that God is going to speak to me. This is what I feel

my part in journaling is: having faith that He has something to say to me, that He will speak to me, and awareness of the state of my soul. Jesus takes it from there!

I have seen Him faithfully meet my faith from being prepared in this way time and time again. Sometimes, there is nothing revelatory or extremely spiritual happening, and I just put down a Scripture I read that somewhat spoke to me while one of my kids was pulling on my shirt, vying for my attention. Other times there is an open heaven, and I can't write all the things God is speaking to me fast enough. Either way, I'm ready.

My mind and flesh are fickle, and I easily forget what God spoke to and promised me and what He carried me through. So, for me, journaling has become my personal memorial stones on this journey with God. I often look back, and my faith is built by reading what He said and promised and how He brought me through hard times. The result is me being completely blown away by His steadfastness and love for me. He is so faithful!

To Pastor Neal's point, early on my journals were like diaries. That's why I painstakingly reviewed them and threw out the diary parts. There was nothing in me that wanted to leave behind something written that would cause pain when read. That's not to say I don't address difficult times and relationships in my journals, because I do. But it's always with the thought to offer it to the Lord and get His perspective, healing, or direction. My journals are guided by a Habakkuk 2:2 principle:

> Then the Lord answered me and said:
> "Write the vision [journal]
> And make *it* plain [handwritten][2] ...

---

2. I believe there is something special about the handwritten word. Having a pen in hand and putting it to paper slows you down and commands your

That when I read it, I will run [hear and obey] with what He is saying to me" (MJP).

Journals are filled with notes taken during messages, sermons, seminars, house groups, and retreats. Then they are reviewed to reflect and further record what God is speaking. I have a fond memory of watching someone mentor their granddaughter in this training. I was seated behind a woman named Barbara Morrison during a church service one day, and she was seated next to her granddaughter Barbie. Barbara slipped a piece of paper and a pen over to Barbie. They both sat there taking notes and recording what they heard God saying to them. I was so impressed at the simple yet profound spiritual discipline this faithful grandmother was passing on to another generation.

While attending Dallas Baptist University, Macey (the daughter of a pastor friend) hit a rough patch. Crucial life decisions had to be made. Night after night she cried out, literally and spiritually, to God. There were more questions than answers. She needed the truth of what He was saying, not the anxious thoughts that plagued her mind. Decisions had to be made!

God knew Macey needed a "When you cry out to Me, I will hear you" breakthrough. She shares:

> It was then Holy Spirit interrupted my internal wrestling and reminded me of a journal of letters I had written years earlier! I found the journal. I reread it. Here on pages written so long ago, God used the same words to give me clarity on

---

full attention. It's deliberate. It's spirit to Spirit. I don't mean to say there is anything wrong with keeping a digital journal, though. I often copy my journal entries over to a digital file so I can later search by topic or by name.

the decision I was facing! This journal became the echoing voice of God that provided me the renewed confidence in trusting God for hard decisions.

This journal Macey refers to was written when she was a young girl. How grateful she is for parents who discipled her and instilled in her the value and blessing of journaling, which reflected her deepening relationship with God as the years went on!

One of the most common questions asked of pastors and spiritual leaders is this: "How do I hear the voice of God for myself?" I used to be very intimidated when I heard other people say, "God told me ..." How could I learn to hear God's voice? Journaling was the answer. Partnered with my Bible, journaling allowed me to begin growing in confidence in hearing God for myself. Then the journals (and notes in my Bible) would confirm God's voice over and over again. When I begin any mentoring relationship, I always begin with, "Bring your Bible and a journal."

Recently, I taught a class on journaling. I covered practical steps on the why and how of recording what God is saying to us. The best (weightiest) part of the class came when I prayed at the end. In the middle of the prayer, I sensed God wanted not just to activate this spiritual discipline in our lives but also to add value to it.

I said, "The day may come when books are confiscated, and Bibles are burned. What is left to tell about the faithfulness of God but our journals?" Even today we hear of the same thing happening in various parts of our world. So I leave that with you to weigh. Our journals are a record of the most valued eternal relationship we have here on earth. Perhaps one day they will live to be an encouragement to others. Each of us will serve as a scribe, recording what God is saying to us!

Blessed *is* he who shall eat bread in the kingdom of God!

Luke 14:15

6

WHAT IF?

> I urge you to offer your bodies as a living and holy sacrifice *to God*, a sacred offering that brings Him pleasure; this is your reasonable, essential worship.
>
> —Romans 12:1 (VOICE)

It was a perfect Grandmother-day. My granddaughters Mackenzie and Bethanie and I were elbow deep in flour, sugar, and sprinkles. Favorite cookie cutters and icing brought out the artist in both girls. Cookies, fresh from the oven, were ready to eat!

As I served the girls their special creations, Mackenzie asked why I wasn't having any. I explained that I was fasting. Puzzled, my granddaughters asked what that was. I told them I was giving up something good (in this instance, food) for something better—prayer. They were intrigued and began to ask me even more questions. I explained that fasting is a special time to pray and hear God, and I described how Jesus and other people in the Bible fasted. Still there were more questions and even more explanations. Mackenzie finally said, "Gege, I don't care what you say. Fasting sounds like being grounded to me!"

That evening the Lord and I had a good laugh. Yes, at times, fasting can seem like being grounded. But as I have walked with the Lord and He has allowed me to participate with Him in fast after fast, I have learned that this discipline is pure joy! Whether surrendering a meal, an activity, or something else, each fast has brought me closer to the heart of the Father. Do I feel grounded? No, I feel anchored. In the midst of life's winds and waves, a fast tethers me to my Savior.

It's been 20-plus years since that sweet baking day with my granddaughters, and I have come to a place where I live a fasting lifestyle. I love to partner with God in breaking through glass prayer ceilings. I love to decrease as He increases in every area of my life. I love to reflect on what He has taught me through denying the soul and building the spirit-man.

Since the global pandemic began, I've been in a "Mary-pondering" zone. It seems as if everything that can be shaken is being shaken. You can hear it on the news and read it on social media posts. The enemy is roaring like a lion, seeking to kill, steal, and destroy. Marriages are dissolving, families are unraveling, and youth suicide rates are at an all-time high. Cultural, social, and political wars are being fought in the courts of public opinion instead of in the throne room of our God. If ever we needed Jesus, we need Him now!

Still, I sense a growing holy dissatisfaction. The praying Church must not be willing to settle! The past few months I have been pondering, processing, and preparing. Then, as we approached the Jewish holiday of Purim last month (March 2022), the Holy Spirit's prodding reached a crescendo. Purim is a feast that remembers Queen Esther's appeal to King Ahasuerus on behalf of her people who were being threatened with annihilation. Esther and her people fasted for three days in preparation for this appeal. Through wisdom, strategy, and the favor of God, Esther saved her people and destroyed the evil plot and plotter (Haman).

For three days the Holy Spirit continued bringing up the subject of Esther and fasting. I recalled the 12-month fast I did in 2010. I revisited the Scriptures of Esther's 12 months of preparation to go before the King—six months of myrrh (death to self) and six months of incense (prayers of the saints). It seemed clear God was inviting me to do another 12-month fast!

I started pacing and praying. I paced myself right down to my second prayer room (my kitchen), put on my apron (my prayer shawl), and lined up my bread ingredients with my mixer (my worship instrument). I was about to prepare an offering to the Lord.

Lost in the wonder of watching the yeast rise after mixing the dough and prayer-kneading it, I knew God was preparing my heart for a 12-month fasting journey. Now, in my experience, fasts reap personal and corporate fruit. I knew this was for me on one level, but on another and perhaps more important level, this was intercession for the Church and our nation. Revival! This fast was for prayer to rise to new levels and break sound barriers and glass ceilings for His kingdom to come on earth as it is in heaven. For me. For us. For generations.

I asked the Lord directly about grace to do this fast and finish well. He took me in a different direction and asked me, "**What if?**" What would-could-should my living prayer life, my physical life, and my spiritual life look like in a year? What if ...?

I always look for a Scripture to confirm God's voice, leading, and nudging. So as my bread was rising, I returned to my prayer room and did a search for "what if." Imagine my shock and awe when I found Abraham's intercession on behalf of a people and a city in Genesis 18!

- Verse 28: *What if* there are five less than fifty?
- Verse 29: *What if* there are forty found there?
- Verse 30: *What if* there are thirty found there?
- Verse 31: *What if* there are twenty found there?
- Verse 32: *What if* there are ten found there?

God is preparing His Intercessors, His Bride, His Church for "What if" prayers!

I shared my thoughts on my social media page and asked if anyone was interested in joining me on their own "What if" journey. The responses amazed me! Here is one from my friend Sandy: "What if we stopped believing the lies of the enemy and started believing the truth?"

The floodgates opened in my mind and spirit:

- What if we stopped giving opinions and sought to offer godly counsel?
- What if we ate right, exercised, and got enough sleep?
- What if we forgave ourselves and stopped focusing on our already-forgiven-by-God sins and failures?
- What if we intentionally spent our time being discipled? Going to school? Reading those books? (Writing those books, too?)
- What if we took this time to submit ourselves to testing, as if God was suggesting, "Test Me on this fast and see what I will do!"?

What is your "What if"? Perhaps you have never fasted, and you aren't sure about it. Well, today is a great day to learn! To begin! Fasting is a wonderful way to have a breakthrough in your relationship with God. We learn to see and hear the Father, Son, and Holy Spirit so clearly when fasting. The enemy knows we are on the praise-warpath, ready to overcome him in every area where he may have tried to sneak in a foothold.

Matthew 6:16 says, "When you fast," not "*If* you decide to fast." Fasting is not optional; it's an expectation. I say that not to condemn anyone but to stir up anticipation and excitement in your spirit! Ask the Lord how, when, and what He would like you to fast. You don't have to jump in to a 12-month fast, unless of course He directs you to do so. Whether it's one meal, one day, one week, or one year, the Holy Spirit will guide, confirm, and direct you every step of the way.

I asked the Lord to show me a single item to give up, but He didn't—at least not outright, anyway. Instead, God wanted it to be something I was willing to give up of my own volition. I had a thought—the most difficult "give up" I could do for a year—but I wanted Him to confirm it in Scripture. And He did! Imagine ... popcorn!

While you are waiting for your "What if?" moment, search the Scriptures for God's principles for fasting. When did the people of God fast, and what was their reason? What was the outcome? There are many books on the subject of fasting, and I recommend starting with Jentezen Franklin's *Fasting: Opening the Door to a Deeper, More Intimate, More Powerful Relationship with God*.[3]

Our desire to fast comes straight from the heart of God. And His "What if?" will always be bigger, wiser, and braver than anything we could think, dream, or imagine.

Father, thank You for giving us such a precious powerful spiritual discipline to come into Your presence and partner with You. Lord Jesus thank you for prioritizing fasting before You began Your earthly ministry. Holy Spirit, show us when, how long,

---

3. Jentezen Franklin, *Fasting: Opening the Door to a Deeper, More Intimate, More Powerful Relationship with God* (Lake Mary, FL: Charisma House, 2008).

and ways to fast. Give us Your heart for "thy kingdom come and thy will be done on earth as it is in heaven" so we can become kingdom-changers through our lifestyle of fasting and prayer.

7

ENOUGH IS ENOUGH

> I thought I could describe a state; make a map of sorrow. Sorrow, however, turns out to be not a state but a process.
>
> —C. S. Lewis, *A Grief Observed*[4]

"**E**nough is enough." The Holy Spirit whispered these three words that began my personal journey into the healing of my very wounded spirit. I was the target of someone's intended blame-game, and I wasn't consciously aware of how deep their false accusations went into my spirit. Still, I knew the arrows had pierced my heart, and I felt a deep breath come out of me when I heard, "Enough is enough." Help was on the way.

Have you ever walked through a time when a loved one or close friend betrayed you? It could have even been someone who doesn't know you well. Accusations were thrown about in casual conversation against you. How about when who you are and what you do were mocked as insincere or self-serving? You may very well have your own story of being on the receiving end of an emotional and spiritual injustice at the hands of a trusted one. Ouch!

---

4. C. S. Lewis, *A Grief Observed*, (New York: HarperOne, 1961), 59.

Although I prefer being the carrier of good news, I must say that if you haven't experienced such heartache, chances are that day will come. None of us are spared the misplaced but well-aimed arrows. From grade school playground bullying to adult social media harassment, arrows are always flying, looking for a target on which to land. Even Jesus dealt with interpersonal turmoil. His family didn't understand His calling. His disciples abandoned Him. The people He came for rejected Him and ultimately crucified Him. "Release Barabbas to us!" they shouted on the fateful day when Pontius Pilate had an eternal decision to make.

Healing can only begin when we acknowledge we are hurt—hurt to the degree we are not ourselves. As we recognize the signs of isolation, depression, anger, anxiety, loss of sleep, and so on, we must be willing to open the wound, address it honestly, and give God opportunities to heal us body, soul, and spirit.

Here are three steps the Holy Spirit walked me through into the fullness of God's healing:

SELF-PITY

   a. Do not allow the spirit of self-pity to take root. Feeling sad is one thing, but crossing the line to feeling sorry for yourself is a red flag.
   b. Avoid nurturing this spirit, coming into agreement with it, or accepting its lies as truths. Otherwise, self-pity will become a stronghold.
   c. Stop those internal conversations that will never take place in the real world.
   d. Grab hold of a Scripture that speaks life over you and the situation. There are so many Scriptures that affirm that God understands and hears your prayers.

e. Resist rehearsing your hurts and digging a deeper grave of offense. Those taunting voices are not God; rather, they are designed by the enemy to provoke you.

Know that God is your Defender. He is for you, not against you. He is your refuge and strong tower. Instead of nurturing the offense, I turned to the One who took my offense for me. I changed my focus. I did not deny the hurt, pain, and injustice; rather, I chose to focus on God rescuing and healing my heartache and deep disappointment.

Beware of the pitfalls that come with offenses. Head them off at the pass. When an incident occurred recently, I journaled. "NO. Not going to let the enemy have one day of my life wallowing in the offense." I put a shield of faith around me that deflected the arrows. I prayed for the ones involved and asked God to move on their hearts and in their lives. I sensed that, like Job, David, and even my Lord Jesus, my reputation was in God's hands.

THE RIGHT QUESTION

You may be familiar with the question Jesus asked Peter: "Who do you say I am?" (Matthew 16:15 NIV). In the most loving and wonderful way, God turned that question on me. And He had me ask the Father, Son, and Holy Spirit, "Who do You say I am?"

I didn't ask just once. No, this became the topic of ceaseless prayer. My quest for an answer to this holy question took weeks and then months. Little by little. Scripture by Scripture. Through the Holy Spirit's whispers and God's voice speaking through others, I began to replace words that wounded with words that healed. Words meant to destroy gave way to words meant to bring life. Accusations targeted at tearing down bowed to affirmations that built me up.

This spiritual exercise was not just something I needed to go through for healing. Rather, God used this time to build into my spirit a strength, a joy, and a knowing that He is *enough. And I'm enough for Him. Enough is enough!*

PRAYER PARTNERS

Ask God for trusted prayer partners who don't seek to counsel, fix, minimize, or amplify the situation. These are people who don't say words merely to make you feel better. No, they go to God on your behalf and ask, "Father, how would You have me pray?" Then they come back with dagger-removers wrapped around Scripture. Now, I am not saying empathy and sympathy are bad. They aren't! But when words are man's and not from God, they simply mask our wound instead of healing it. One word, one Scripture, or one truth from God is worth an encyclopedia of well-meaning and loving words from friends.

My healing began by acknowledging to myself that there were daggers. I could no longer deny the hurt that is often accompanied by righteous anger. I had to be willing to open the wound so it could heal. This can be complicated, and depending on the who, how, what, where, and when, your healing may require the help of a professional counselor. What I've shared here are not the only ways to heal from a wounded spirit, but they are prayer principles foundational to gaining and keeping your spiritual health.

So if the Son makes you free, then you are unquestionably free (John 8:36 AMP).

You have been traveling around this mountain country long enough. Turn northward (Deuteronomy 2:3 ESV).

The Lord is near to the brokenhearted
    and saves the crushed in spirit (Psalm 34:18 ESV).

Behold, how good and how pleasant *it is*
For brethren to dwell together in unity! (Psalm 133:1).

But he knows the way that I take;
When He has tested me, I shall come forth as gold (Job 23:10).

Father, I believe Romans 8:28—that You work all things for good for those who love You and are called according to Your purpose. That's me! I love You, and I am called to Your purposes for my life. I trust You, Lord Jesus, Rapha-Healer, to provide me with the spiritual and emotional strength not only to withstand but also to walk free from this wound. Holy Spirit, my Counselor, Teacher, and Comforter, Your intercession for me will cause me to break through by resisting, rebuking, and renouncing every scheme, every dagger, and every arrow from the enemy to rob me of even one day of freedom in Christ! Amen.

8

FROM STALE TO SANCTIFIED

> Now to Him who is able to keep you from stumbling,
> And to present *you* faultless
> Before the presence of His glory with exceeding joy.
>
> —Jude 24

It was January 1st—that clean slate, new beginnings, anything-is-possible day. Such a day brings fresh promises, commitments, hopes, and dreams. Reflecting on the new, I remembered a prayer call I had listened to a few days earlier. Thousands of homes across the United States paused to participate in communion—each of us in our individual homes yet corporately preparing to partake of the elements representing Jesus' body and blood. Even over the phone, there was a definite sense of being on holy ground.

Following communion, the host spoke these words: "You have crossed over. Even as with Moses and the children of Israel, the horse and the riders of the past are being cut off by the sea coming in over them. The horse and the riders of your past on this day are cut off. I call you blessed."

> I will sing to the Lord,
> For He has triumphed gloriously!
> The horse and its rider
> He has thrown into the sea! (Exodus 15:1).

Days later, that declaration still resonated in my spirit. I found myself rehearsing a lament: "Lord, really? The enemy (horse and rider) cut off? Into the sea? I need proof. I need a sign from You, an assurance I cannot deny."

There are times in our walk with the Lord when we say, "Wait! These sins have been chasing me long enough." We carry a burden that is breaking us rather than an anointing that is breaking the yoke. We've all been there, and many of us remain stuck there. Unforgiveness. Anger. Sadness. Confusion. Hurt. Broken relationships—even a relationship with ourselves. Oh, that cycle of being able to forgive others but not ourselves!

These are those besetting sins Scripture addresses in Hebrews. They are the sins we constantly struggle with and have a weakness toward. They easily entangle us. These thoughts, words, and deeds separate us from experiencing God's presence and all His attributes—peace, joy, love, goodness, mercy, etc. Instead, they come in like a flood, distorting and dominating our thoughts, opinions, and attitudes about ourselves. These are the places we fight to keep the door closed to Satan and his demons so they cannot attack and wound us.

So there I was, fresh into what I prayed was truly a new day in this brand-new year. Anchored in my prayer chair, I placed my heart under the microscope of the Holy Spirit. I was looking for that blessed assurance that I was forgiven and that the horse and riders were thrown into the sea. I rehearsed the besetting sin I had long dealt with and received my God's forgiveness. But forgiving myself was another matter altogether. I kept reminding the Father of how I saw myself. I felt very much like the woman in the Bible who was being stoned, except the accuser was me!

Perhaps you have had similar thoughts:

- "I have done irreparable damage."
- "God can never use me again."
- "He is disappointed in me."

Isn't that just like the devil, the accuser of the saints? He loves to remind us of things the Lord has already thrown into the sea of forgetfulness and make it harder to forgive ourselves than to forgive others.

I had a thought, one that came from a deep desire: *I want to take communion*. I had made some challah the day earlier. Perfect! I went to retrieve the loaf, but I couldn't find it anywhere. I asked my husband, Bruce, about the bread. He said he had thrown it away because it was dried up and stale.

Refusing to be deterred, I went digging through the trash. There, buried beneath coffee grounds and leftovers, was my communion bread. I rescued it and with careful precision began cutting off the damaged parts. One side. Two sides. Three sides. Four sides. Five sides. Six sides. What was left of the triple braided challah loaf was a one-inch white square of *beautiful, spotless* bread. The bread had been redeemed!

Returning to my prayer chair, I prayed over the bread. I sensed the Lord's familiar whisper saying, "Mary, this is how I see you. Not dirt, trash, ruined, damaged, thrown out, unusable. This is how I want you to see yourself." Just then the precision of the Holy Spirit took my questioning, wounded heart and cut off the accusations that clung to it like barnacles on a ship.

I chose water for communion. My prayer was that God would make new wine in me. I asked Him to transform my troubled, wounded, and heavy heart into a new wineskin—one prepared to hold, embrace, and run with the new line-in-the-sand, crossing-over-into-my-promised-land plans God has for me. I thanked the Lord for throwing my horse and rider into the sea of forgetfulness.

Like the food from heaven provided for the going-around-the-mountain again Israelites, the Lord, in His goodness, provided *manna* for my communion. And Jesus, the Bread of Life (John 6:22) and Word of God (John 1:1), in communion with the Holy Spirit, set this captive free.

Friend, what about you? Is your relationship with God bogged down, dried up, or lacking in two-way conversation? Are you wanting to walk free from a besetting sin? Are you struggling with accepting God's forgiveness or forgiving yourself?

I assure you this is not God's will for you. In fact, the Scriptures remind us through the lives of others like David, Abraham, and Paul that God wants us to walk in that blessed assurance we are His. And we can be truly set free from the accuser's harassing, tormenting voice.

My pastor recently spoke about grace and forgiving ourselves. When he was wrestling with post-salvation sin, God told him, "The failure you committed after you got saved is under the blood like the failures you committed before you got saved. You need to forgive yourself. You received grace when you came to Christ, but you need to receive grace today." Today, receive God's grace to walk fully forgiven and free to be all He created you to be.

Allow God to direct your heart. For me, breakthrough came in the form of a communion experience. It may be the same for you, or it may be different. Whatever it is, decide that today will be your breakthrough. The horse and rider are drowned! Walk with me into tomorrow unhindered and free.

> For the law was given through Moses; grace and truth came through Jesus Christ (John 1:17 NIV).

> What are you, you great mountain? Before Zerubbabel *you will become* a plain; and he will bring out the top stone *with* shouts of "Grace, grace to it!" (Zechariah 4:7 NASB).

> Then Peter came to Jesus and asked, "Lord, how many times shall I forgive my brother or sister who sins against me? Up to seven times?"
> Jesus answered, "I tell you, not seven times, but seventy-seven times" (Matthew 18:21–22 NIV).

> You have circled this mountain long enough. *Now* turn north (Deuteronomy 2:3 NASB).

Father, I know Your will for my life is to live under grace, not law. Jesus, I know You came to fulfill the law and give me grace-filled forgiveness. Holy Spirit, I know that in my weaknesses, You have become my strength. Today I choose to cross over to my promised land of forgiveness. I forgive myself and move forward to live for Your glory. In Jesus' name, Amen.

9

TENDING YOUR FIELDS

I fell in love with a farmer. Ole McBrucie had a farm in Ohio where he raised wheat. One beautiful, romantic evening when the harvest moon was shining brightly, we sat on the hood of his truck, and I served him homemade meatloaf, mashed potatoes, and green beans. Bruce was harvesting wheat, but I was sowing seeds for a happy, he-loves-my-cooking husband! Forty-four blessed, married years later, we still speak of that meal as being our favorite.

At the time, I was a new follower of Christ falling in love with the Word of God. I heard a message on Matthew 13:18–23 that deeply moved me. The now familiar parable is about the sower and the seed and what could happen to that seed if it isn't planted in good soil and cared for properly.

Surrounded by fields and seeds, barns and storehouses, tractors and combines, and lots of good soil, God was about to teach me eternal lessons about stewarding His Word (seed). He was making certain that my heart was good soil to receive the seeds of the Word and that I would tend and care for it so there would be a harvest. In my life. In my prayer life. In my ministry to the Lord and others. Already the Spirit of God was rising in me, and I declared, "No, Satan and his demons will *not* steal, trample, or destroy this precious, beloved, and holy Word of God from me. It is the truth that sets me free and keeps me free. There will be a harvest of living a life that brings God glory. No, this seed is my seed!" I knew God would give me revelation, understanding, and life applications.

During the next planting season, the crops were coming up, and they were so beautiful. I loved watching the wind blow through the rows of grain because it reminded me of a wave offering to the Lord. Early one morning—yes, it's true that farmers keep very early mornings—I looked out the kitchen window. There was Bruce, walking up the hill to the fields with our golden retriever following close behind. Bruce was carrying a huge black garbage bag and a set of shears. I didn't see him again until almost dinnertime. That's when I learned what he had been doing. He was walking through the eight acres, row by row, looking for Johnsongrass, a weed that would choke out his crop and damage the soil. He removed the weed by the root and bagged it so no bad seed would fall on good soil.

We know wheat and weeds (tares) represent a kingdom principle for the Church. In a parable, Jesus demonstrates how important it is for us not to allow weeds to contaminate or ruin our seed in our field (His harvest). If there is something choking out the Word of God in our attitudes, relationships, words, or actions, our hearts can become deceived and wicked, stony and cold, or wounded and broken. We must not allow any bitter or twisted lie or scheme of the enemy to take root.

> Lord, I pray You would uproot any and all seeds that would damage, destroy, or delay the work of God, the love of God, or the ministry of Holy Spirit in my life.

Let's look at our fields and ask ourselves some questions:

- Where are we planted?
- Where and with whom do we have influence?
- Where is God thriving in our lives?
- Where are there weeds?

After we identify our fields (yes, there can be more than one), we need to talk about seeding them.

Good seeds are the foundation of a great harvest. Zechariah 8:12 speaks of seeds that shall prosper. God is giving good seeds (gifts) to the sower (you and me). The primary seed is the Word of God, but there are also different kinds of seeds that are the gifts God gives us to produce a harvest. These seeds include faith, forgiveness, longsuffering, joy, kindness, discernment, wisdom, and prophecy. When we consider the seeds God is giving us, we think of natural and supernatural gifts. We reap what we sow, and we will reap a harvest if we don't grow weary!

Isaiah 28:23–29 (MSG) speaks of farmers who plow, prepare, and plant.

> They know exactly what to do and when to do it.
> Their God is their teacher (v. 26).

> The farmer knows how to treat each kind of grain.
> He's learned it all from God-of-the-Angel-Armies,
> who knows everything about when and how and where
> (vv. 28–29).

What I love about these verses is that each seed needs to be treated differently. Just as a seed of corn must be treated differently than a seed of wheat, so too must spiritual seeds be uniquely handled. The Holy Spirit is the one who will guide us in sowing the right seed at the right time, praying over that seed, and fasting, believing, and worshipping as we water it.

Wow! Take heart, saints. We do not have to figure out this farming, planting, plowing, watching over, and harvesting all by ourselves. God will teach us how to treat each kind of seed because each seed needs to be treated differently.

I picture a crop duster airplane, like the Holy Spirit, flying low over your field and seeding you with everything you need for the harvest. "For soil that drinks the rain which often falls on it and produces crops useful to those for whose benefit it is cultivated, receives a blessing from God" (Hebrews 6:7 AMP).

Saints, others will glean in our fields. God will send people who need to learn how to gather and plant their own fields. I once was part of a pastoral team visiting Switzerland. We met up with a family whose ministry was based in a farming community. They were so inspired by the teachings they received on building houses of prayer that they shared them with local farmers. One farmer undeniably took the principles to heart—he consecrated his farm to the Lord, and his fields became a "house of prayer." He prayed over each aspect of tending his fields. God gave him prayer direction, wisdom, and the insight needed to oversee and care for the seeds, the crops, and the harvest. Lo and behold, this farmer had a huge harvest! And the potatoes he grew were so big that he could not sell them commercially (they could not be processed through traditional machines). He had to sell them at an organic farmers' market, substantially increasing his profits— all from the spiritual seeds from the teachings sown just a few months earlier.

As we steward the Word of God in our lives, tend to our field, and go about the Father's business, we will be leaving fields for others. One morning God dropped the words *wide pasture* into the middle of our conversation. I searched for this phrase in Scripture, and I found only one verse that had the words *wide* and *pasture* in it—1 Chronicles 4:40. You're going to love this! It's about a well-tended pasture that was enjoyed by others who moved there. I added my personal application in parenthesis:

> They (the generations that follow) found rich, good pasture, and the [cleared] land was wide, quiet, and peaceful, because the people of Ham (you and me) had dwelt there of old [and had left it a better place for those who came after them]. (They were good, obedient stewards of My Word, the gifts I gave them, and My presence) (AMP and MJP).

The following is my journal entry from the Father. I wrote it in red ink, which I use whenever I hear His voice.

> Mary, tend the "field" (wide pasture) I am giving you. I will instruct you how to use each gift I'm giving you so those who follow will find a rich, good, peaceful pasture to dwell in—a field planted where My presence will dwell.

God will indeed tell us how to care for each seed, naturally and spiritually! Saints, you are good soil. The Word of God is taking root. The fields you have sown will continue to yield fruit season after season. And you will reap the fruit that others will toil to produce from fields you've planted, as will the generations to follow.

10

I LAY CLAIM TO YOUR EVENINGS

He must increase, but I *must* decrease.

—John 3:30

When people interrupt you mid-sentence, it can feel a bit bothersome. Are they not listening to you? Do they not care what you have to say? Is something you're saying offending them? This happened to me one morning, and interestingly enough, it happened when I was talking to the Lord. I had a lot on my mind, and out of the clear, pre-dawn morning I heard, "I lay claim to your evenings." What? Where did that come from? Surely not me! After all, my evenings have traditionally been a time to unwind with an oversized bowl of parmesan popcorn and some mindless activity. Needlework. Social media scrolling. Favorite home decorating or cooking TV program. The evenings were my time! *Gulp.* "I lay claim to your evenings."

However, this holy interruption, unlike many person-to-person ones, delivered a peace and a "this is settled" feeling in my heart. Not only was God interrupting my conversation with something more important to Him (and ultimately to me), but

He was also about to interrupt my calendar—my day-to-day, or rather day-to-night, routine. You see, I am what the dictionary and everyone else would describe as nocturnal. I wake up at 10 pm. I like the peace and quiet of the sleeping house. I treasure and, if truth be told, covet *my* evening time. It's in those late-night hours that my unfinished to-do list fades into a compartmentalized, Scarlett O'Hara "I'll think about it tomorrow" place. After all, tomorrow is another day.

How about your evenings? Are you like my husband who keeps farmers' hours, early to bed and early to rise? Or are your evenings your most productive times, when your creative juices start flowing?

I came to learn that the point God was making with me was that my late evenings are just as important to Him as our treasured pre-dawn mornings. Also, He knew how compromised my body and soul were when my nights were too short and my days were too long. He had heard my endless prayer pleas of "Make me a morning person." I just didn't realize making me a morning person would mean changing my evenings.

I recorded the following in my journal with a red pen:

> Mary,
> Your nights are as much mine as your mornings.
> The stillness and hush of evening as much as the
> stillness and hush of early pre-dawn mornings.
> I lay claim to your evenings.

Then to add value to what God was challenging and charging me with, He sent me traveling through the Scriptures. I thought, *Why do the Jewish people begin their "days" at sundown the night before?* That always confused me. But then I found Genesis 1:5: "God called the light Day, and the darkness He called Night. So the evening and the morning were the first day." That required a little mind twist for me. It seemed upside down. And then this whisper:

> Mary,
> Sundown—evening—is the beginning of our day.
> You are my invited guest.
> Plan accordingly.
> Love, Abba

With such an invitation, how could I not?!

Months have passed since that topsy-turvy God-interruption. Has it been easy? No. Long-held habits are not easily broken. Has it been successful? Not every evening. In fact, I had to write, "I lay claim to your evenings" on a piece of paper and tape it to my bathroom mirror. I had to put a calendar reminder in my phone. I had to rearrange my bedside table. I had to say no to some evening commitments. I had to take some practical, pragmatic, and often problematic steps to make the switch.

Has it been worth it? Oh my, yes! But I've learned that God doesn't ask anything of me that doesn't have a blessing attached to it. How about you? Has God interrupted or tried to interrupt your conversation? Your calendar? Your commitments? Does He have a "more" He wants to do for, with, or through you?

Two Scriptures have been my yes and amen to this God-shift. For my evenings:

> Let my prayer be counted as incense before You;
> The lifting up of my hands as the evening offering
> (Psalm 141:2 AMP).

For my mornings:

> As for me, Father, because of Jesus' righteousness
> and my right standing with You,
> I will be fully satisfied, when I awake in the morning,
> seeing You face-to-face and having sweet communion with You
> (Psalm 17:15 MJP).

Maybe it's not your evenings. Maybe it's your mornings. Or perhaps a zone-out routine that has been more of an escape-from than an engage-in. Ask God if there is something, someone, or some specific time He is wanting to rearrange in your life. As John the Baptist said of Jesus in John 3, there must be more of Him and less of us. He must increase, and we must decrease. To God be the glory!

God, who watches over me and keeps me day and night, I feel Your tugging at my heart. The dictionary defines claim as "to take as the rightful owner; to assert to be rightfully one's own."[5] That's truth, Lord. You do have every right to own and possess and lay claim to any part of my life—my heart, my plans, my time, etc. Today, by the power of the Holy Spirit, strengthen me to resolve, to hear, and to obey. I submit to Your claim to all of me. In Jesus' name, Amen.

---

5. *Merriam-Webster.com Dictionary*, s.v. "claim," accessed March 30, 2022, https://www.merriam-webster.com/dictionary/claim.

Jesus was recognized by them when he broke the bread.

Luke 24:35 NIV

11

SABBATH: A CHECKUP
My Story

> O my soul! Return *and relax. Come* to your *true* rest,
> for the Eternal has showered you with His favor.
> —Psalm 116:7 (VOICE)

It's Friday evening. How fitting that I would be writing to you about Sabbath. The aroma of freshly baked bread fills my home and heart. The sun is about to set on another week. And the anticipated, looked-forward-to gift of time has arrived.

There's so much I want to tell you about this special day. There's so much the Holy Spirit has taught me over the past 11 years. This gift of time, more than any other spiritual discipline, has singularly impacted my life of prayer and touched every area of my life and relationships. My deepest desire is to communicate the essence of Sabbath and the gift it is to you. So lean in, read with your mind, and listen with your heart.

Let's begin with a little context. In my growing up years, "Sabbath" meant we went to church on Sunday and took the rest of the day off. As I reflect on that time, it didn't have the "keep it holy" element to the day. Then, when I surrendered my life in Christ, there was an inborn desire to grow in spiritual disciplines. I just didn't think Sabbath was one of them. Although there were covered dishes to be eaten after church, the time was more about food and fellowship than a biblical commandment.

Fast forward to 2011. I was full-time, head-over-heels in love with being part of a church staff. My duties included serving in weekend (Saturday and Sunday) services. Instead of Sabbath becoming more holy, it became busier! I elected to make Friday evening to Saturday evening my Sabbath. I simply filled those hours and days with more activity. One tired, burned-out, and overcommitted morning I cried out to God, "There has got to be a better way to serve You with passion and purpose!"

My spiritual, physical, and emotional checkup that morning resulted in a dire diagnosis of an unsustainable rhythm in my body, soul, and spirit. And it wasn't because I was working full-time on our church staff. Each of us is "full-time," whether we are stay-at-home parents, business leaders, students, entrepreneurs, spouses, singles ... the list could go on. The only requirement to full-time ministry is a life surrendered to Jesus.

The problem was my passion ran ahead of God's purposes. My calendar ran me instead of me running my calendar. Have you ever experienced something like that? When our yeses are unsanctified (more us than God). When we worry instead of sleep. When our bodies and souls run on fumes, not fuel. When our spiritual address is hope-deferred. When our families live disconnected, leaving everyone wanting more. When we find ourselves saying, "As soon as this project is completed, or game season is behind us, or the holidays are over ..." When we make the excuses, "There's never enough time. I'm so tired. I'm too busy," we become the perfect candidates for God to interrupt our lives with the gift of time.

It's time for a Sabbath checkup, and the first thing is to get past the contrariness of it all:

- I'm about to make an appeal for you to prayerfully consider dedicating 24 hours and making your Sabbath holy, but you're telling me you don't have enough time as it is!
- I'm going to encourage you to make plans for a special Sabbath meal, but you're telling me that getting the family together for a meal is already a big project.
- I'm going to urge you to clear your mind of your endless to-do lists and trust they will be taken care of in spite of—or rather, *because of*—taking a day called Sabbath.

That momentous morning when I lamented to God, seeking help for my mental, emotional, and physical state, was my wake-up call. I realized I had just completed an extended vacation and should be refreshed, renewed, and ready to go! Instead, I was seriously questioning whether I could get back on the same bus (or under it) without a genuine God-intervention. It was clear I needed more of Him and less of me to move forward. It was clear something had to change.

In the past, I considered saying more noes. I thought about ways to get more rest and exercise. I had cried to my husband and prayer partners for wisdom, insight, and counsel. In fact, on one occasion a dear friend leaned forward, asked, "May I be so bold?" and proceeded to try and get me off the runaway train I had been on for so long. I hadn't really listened then, but on this particular morning, God interrupted me with one word: *rest*.

I searched for "rest" on the internet, and the first result was a book by Congressman Joe Lieberman (a religiously observant Jew) titled *The Gift of Rest*. I downloaded the book, and on the first page I began reading a quote from the Talmud: "The Holy

One Blessed Be He." The. Holy. One. Blessed. Be. He. I paused. This phrase took my breath away. I know in this time of church history when we focus on an intimate relationship with God, we use family names like Papa, Abba, and Daddy. Yet in that moment the Holy Spirit rested on this phrase, and I worshipped in awe.

Then I read:

> Moses, in my storehouse I have a goodly gift,
> and the Sabbath is its name.
> —Talmud, Beitzah 16a

The Holy Spirit whispered, "Mary, if you'll learn to Sabbath, you'll go another lap!"

I was about to learn that God's rest is not a calendar, commitment, or sleep issue at all. Rather, it's all about discovering how to live on God's time. His pace and rhythm. His "come to me, all you who are weary." His desire is for you and me to be equally yoked to Him. I knew at that moment God and I were embarking on another prayer adventure, but little did I know that my quest to observe the Sabbath would enrich every area of my life, every day of my week, and every part of my relationship with God Himself.

A new adventure in a life of prayer was about to begin. And I was all in as I cried out, "Teach me, Lord."

Throughout this book, we will take time to consider and ask God what Sabbath looks like in our busy lives. Here is just a start to the journey:

- What does Sabbath currently look like in your life?
- What does God want Sabbath to look like in your life?
- What distinguishes these 24 hours from the rest of the week?

- What boundaries (Psalm 16:5–6) do you need to place around Sabbath that will make this day a pleasant place? Holy?

Please don't disqualify yourself as a candidate for God's ordained and anointed plan to live a life of rest. It's yours for the taking! Will it require adjusting your calendar, your mindset, and life as you've known it? Yes. Will it be worth it? Yes!

For now, rest in knowing God has a plan for your Sabbath. And as the prophet Jeremiah reminds us, God's plans are "for good and not for disaster, to give you a future and a hope" (Jeremiah 29:11 NLT).

And rest in these truths:

> Then Jesus said, "Come to me, all of you who are weary and carry heavy burdens, and I will give you rest" (Matthew 11:28 NLT).
>
> And he said to them, "The Sabbath was made for man, not man for the Sabbath" (Mark 2:27 ESV).
>
> So then, there remains a Sabbath rest for the people of God (Hebrews 4:9 ESV).

Lord, the idea of Sabbath is not new to me. Applying it to my life, changing my mindset, rearranging my calendar, and trusting You for it is! I acknowledge there is more to the commandment, this gift of rest, than I can comprehend. I'm willing. And You're able. Amen.

12

A DIVINE INVITATION

God has a plan.
We have a prayer.
God has a purpose.
We have a prayer.
God has a process.
We have a prayer.

God desires to set us up for divine appointments. "What is a divine appointment?" you may ask. Some might call it being in the right place at the right time. However, I prefer to think of it as being in a God-anointed place at a God-appointed time. These are the moments in which hindsight clearly demonstrates that God had a plan, and we were carrying His presence into the situation. We don't just show up to these moments; no, we are sent to them.

Such was the case when I received an invitation for a drive-by, N-95 masked, wave-from-the-car baby shower. These celebrations were popular during the 2020 pandemic as people had to isolate from each other. It would have been understandable to send a regret, a gift, and a note. My dear friends certainly would have understood. However, after receiving the invitation, I had an inexplicable desire to go. To participate. To be present.

It turns out God was setting me and the couple up for His preordained appointment. Even the timing of my arrival could be described as a *moed,* a Hebrew word for an 'appointed time.' Bruce and I pulled up to their home just in time to watch the last car pull away. There on the driveway, filled with leftover refreshments and delivered gifts, stood the expectant couple and their five-year-old daughter, Maggie Jean.

They are very special couple to me. Benjamin, accompanied by his wife, Jenni, had been my worship leader on a Prayer-Worship Encounter Tour in Israel about six years earlier. That trip was a divine appointment! While in Shiloh (where Hannah cried out to God for a son), God gave them the name of their prayed-for, hoped-for, and dreamed-of son: Levi Samuel. Shortly after returning home, they discovered their second divine appointment: Jenni was pregnant! Fully expecting this baby to be the son God named, they could not have been more surprised nine months later when their precious *daughter*, Maggie Jean, was born!

It's their story to tell in full, but I do have permission to say the pregnancy and delivery with Maggie Jean were difficult. Jenni's body took years to recover, and doctors were unsure if she would ever be able to get pregnant again. Five years later, they were thrilled to be pregnant once again, and this time, they were preparing to meet their long-awaited baby boy!

Jenni, now great with child, was beaming. What was supposed to be a quick gift-drop off and air-hug turned into a Simeon and Anna prayer moment. (Luke 2:25–38 tells of their divine appointment praying over baby Jesus and sharing the good news of His birth.) Jenni indeed was carrying their named-in-Israel son. Levi means "joined to God," and Samuel means "God hears." During the pregnancy the name Ernest, which means "well-born," also kept coming up. Benjamin and Jenni prayerfully declared that this baby's delivery would not include the body-wrecking havoc the young mom had previously endured. They were clinging to that name and promise for their son, Levi Samuel Ernest.

Looking at Jenni, I felt an "instant prayer" weight fall on me. I asked if I could lay hands on her "promise" and pray. I began and then paused because I sensed God saying, "Let Me pray. Let Me declare over this one. Let me declare 'an inheritance ... having been predestined (chosen, appointed beforehand)'" (Ephesians 1:11 AMP). I obeyed. Then I prayed a brief but spirit-weighty prayer that had the breath of God on it. I prayed their son would carry a finishing anointing like Jesus' finished work on the cross. Many people begin things but do not finish. This son, however, would have an apostolic (establishing) finishing anointing. We all felt the presence of God hovering over the end of the driveway as we participated in this heaven-to-earth prayer meeting.

With tears in his eyes, Benjamin confirmed my prayer: "I cannot tell you how grateful I am that you came by. I had no idea how much I needed to see you. The prayer you prayed was in agreement with a desire so deep inside of me that I didn't know it was there until you prayed it." Thank you, Lord, for divine prayer appointments and obedience!

That simple prayer encounter brought peace to this couple. It was a blessed assurance that God was with them from the beginning and would be with them throughout this delivery. It served as a confirmation that He had not forgotten His Word or promise from those all years ago.

Now, dear readers, this is my story as well as Benjamin and Jenni's story, but ultimately it is yours too. God wants to use this upside-down world full of out-of-our-control circumstances to release intentional, instant prayers. He is turning ordinary, routine, and unplanned moments into divine appointments. He is highlighting how involved He wants to be in our every detail, every desire, and every day! He is unlocking agreeing-with-heaven prayers in you and me!

I believe the Holy Spirit is highlighting the intrinsic value and importance of praying with others in *real time*. Sending an emoji and a quick "I'll pray for you" via text isn't wrong, but there is real power in allowing the Holy Spirit to form the words out loud as you are praying together with other believers.

When I had COVID-19 recently, I asked several friends to send me audio prayers. The sound of their voices comforted me, and the power of their words increased my faith, quieted my fears, and ultimately brought healing to my body. One prayer in particular had a key to my healing that was confirmed by my doctor.

God wants to strengthen the body of Christ by intentionally bringing us together to agree with Him and each other. That's powerful. Let's do it!

Your prayers are a conduit of God's love. I'm urging you to be very sensitive to any nudge from the Holy Spirit to pray instant, immediate prayers. First responder prayers. Short prayers. Spirit-led prayers. In season prayers. Obedient prayers. Destiny prayers. You can do it!

We never know what words of encouragement, comfort, love, and affirmation are going to come out of our mouths when the Lord speaks through us. When we allow His presence, His plan, and His purpose into our lives to accomplish His will, miracles happen, and then He gets all the glory!

The Spirit of the Lord, the Eternal, is on us.
> *The Lord has appointed us for a special purpose.*
He has anointed us to bring good news to the poor.
> He has sent us to repair broken hearts
And to declare to those who are held captive and bound in prison,
> "Be free *from your imprisonment!*" (Isaiah 61:1–3 MJP, taken from the VOICE)

13

A FAITH-TRIP TO THE AIRPORT

It's been said that prayer is more caught than taught. There's a lot of truth to that statement. We are mentored in prayer when we listen to other people praying. They use Scriptures, they address God in a personal way, and they speak with authority and confidence. We catch on and try to do something similar. However, "caught" prayer can leave us longing. "I wish I could, but I can't." "They do, but I don't." We can get caught up in comparison as we attempt to pray our own powerful, effective, and righteous prayers.

There is also prayer that's taught. We can learn so much from equipping classes and resources (I pray this book is one!) that teach principles backed up with Scriptures and stories. However, this "taught" prayer can leave us longing too, with information that fills our heads and hearts but gets stuck without personal application.

Then there's prayer that's lived out loud. This kind of prayer becomes not just what you say but also who you are! This prayer brings God into every day, every detail, and every decision. It binds us to His heart and looses us to be His hands and feet.

Several years ago, my family from Michigan (Anthony and Melissa Geers) faced a judicial nightmare. An unjust, unwarranted, and unrighteous response to a baby's bruised rib turned into an emotional, mental, physical, and financial crisis! Learning how to pray through this traumatic ordeal required staying focused on what God was saying to pray, not what the circumstances were shouting.

It took the Matthew 21:21 kind of faith:

> Truly I say to you, if you have faith and do not doubt, you will not only do what was done to the fig tree, but even if you say to this mountain, "Be taken up and cast into the sea," it will happen (NASB).

Otherwise, we would have drowned day after day as we came up against the lawyers, the judges, the courts, and the social services officials. It required dealing on a day-to-day basis with the reality of walking through this and at the same time calling on our God to intervene, bring justice, and deliver our family.

Throughout the three-month ordeal, the Holy Spirit was showing us how to pray. I had a vision of the judge and lawyers convening in chambers (you can read more about that in the chapter "Lion that Roars"), and at one moment, the Lord had me declare, "No cause! No cause! No cause!" Shortly after, a medical official who was reviewing the case said, "No cause!" These were faith-building times of breakthrough. Nothing had changed in the natural, but we all knew God was engaged and working on our behalf to untangle this legal web that had become a nightmare.

During this time, the Lord impressed me to enlist a dear family of prayer warriors to fight with us. Zach Neese was a worship pastor at our church, and his wife, Jen, was a prayer-intercessor leader and teacher on my team. They and their six children, ages 5 to 15, had partnered with me in several mountain-moving prayer assignments. I marveled watching these young people worship, pray, and cry out to God from a place of such purity. It made me want to have what they had!

And a little boy will lead them (Isaiah 11:6 NASB).

Let no one look down on your youthfulness, but *rather* in speech, conduct, love, faith, *and* purity, show yourself an example of those who believe (1 Timothy 4:12 NASB).

Zach and Jen have taught their children how to worship and how to war. And it's not just "taught" or even "caught"—they live prayer out loud together as a family. This is part of their family ethos. It is who they are. Zach and Jen have modeled for the children the power of corporate prayer and not just how to cry out to God but also how to hear God. And how to obey!

The Neeses had been praying for my family since the crisis happened. One day Zach sent me a picture of the children laying prostrate and kneeling in a circle on their living room floor. It wasn't long afterwards that their daughter Charis came out of her bedroom to share what God has spoken to her. She had been crying for the family, and her empathic heart, which looked and sounded just like Jesus, hurt. She prayed, "Jesus, if You can walk on water, You can do this!" Another daughter, Maggie, prayed, "If You raised Lazarus from the dead after four days, You can do this." Their faith to move this mountain was palatable and powerful.

I received a text from Zach: "Where does your family live? What city? I'll explain later." The next text was, "Thanks. Waiting at the airport." Charis had the impression and unction that they should go to the airport—all eight family members in tow—and sit at the departure gate for the city closest to my family's home. She wanted to go up there and pray with, encourage, and love on them. She believed breakthrough was coming.

They sat at the airport. Throughout the day and into the evening, they went to each gate that had a flight leaving for the destination city, waiting for someone to offer them eight tickets. Even while writing this, I'm blown away at their boldness, courage, and obedience. They were not dissuaded by voices that would mock, question, laugh at, or argue about practicality.

The picture Jen sent of the six children sitting in the lounge dressed and ready to go was one I'll never forget. When the last flight departed, they returned home. But they were not dejected, because they did their part. Charis heard from God. The family came into agreement, one and all, and they obeyed God in this faith-exercise-adventure.

A few days later I received a text from a family member. "It's over. The lawyer just called us. All charges dropped." Did I wail? Did I weep? Oh, yes! We all did. A projected no-end-in-sight legal battle had come to a dramatic, no-cause ending. As quickly as it began, it was over. The lawyers were as shocked as anyone. News reporters gathered on the front lawn with the reunited family to hear of the goodness and faithfulness of a God who hears prayers and moves to action.

I was quick to phone the Neeses. They may not have physically boarded that airplane to minister to and pray with the family in person, but there is no question in anyone's mind that their faith-activated trip to the airport moved that legal mountain.

There were many moving pieces in this story, not the least of which was the baby's mother who turned over every rock, knocked on every door, and contacted any and all officials. There were others who believed and fought on the legal side. Multitudes prayed. Friends and strangers came alongside to do what they could do. As in every prayer assignment, we are just required to do what God asks us to. In the case of Charis and her family, that involved an act of faith and a trip to the airport.

Father, we are inspired by the faith of young children who do not question radical faith living. And we're grateful for those who are training them up. Father, Your Word tells us to come to You as little children. So today we come to You, asking You to train us up in the way we should go! We have caught, and we have been taught, but now is the time for living our prayers out loud. Lord Jesus, we want to be Your feet, Your hands, and an extension of Your heart as when You walked here on earth. Holy Spirit, inspire and empower us to live prayer out loud! Give us opportunities. Give us occasions. Give us prayer assignments. Trust us, Lord God, with faith that will move mountains. In Jesus' name, Amen.

14

BROKEN
Not All Who Wander Are Lost

I really don't like the word *prodigal*. Please don't get upset with me! I understand how it is used in teaching Luke 15:11–32, and I know there are books written, sermons preached, and prayers prayed on the subject. But words matter. If you look up the word "prodigal" in Scripture, you'll only find it in the section heading for the parable.[6] When you look up the definition, you'll find the words "extravagant" and "wasteful."

My heart aches for the "prodigals" in my life and in yours because there's a broken relationship between them and God. Brokenness causes people do things that are contrary to God's nature and plans for us.

When I saw a wooden sign that read, "Not all who wander are lost," I bought it and put it in my prayer room. The word "lost" seems so hopeless. And no one who has wandered from God, who has resisted His love, forgiveness, mercy, and kindness, is hopeless.

---

6. I did find a single exception in the Modern English Version, which reads, "Not many days later, the younger son gathered everything together, and journeyed to a distant country, and there squandered his possessions in prodigal living" (Luke 15:13).

When I'm in my car and I turn down a wrong road, I'm not lost—I'm wandering. (And wondering how to get back on the right road!) There's a difference! And today, right now, I want to declare that God's plan for His sons and daughters is that all who wander find their way home. After all, Jesus said, "I am the way, the truth, and the life" (John 14:6). He's the GPS for all those who are wandering!

I know this might come down to semantics, but it's not just people who are wandering from the truth. It's churches, ministries, and nations too. Consider the Israelites during their 40 years in the wilderness. Those are not called the lost years; those are the wandering years. Those are the years when God was breaking through and healing the brokenness from bondage (Egypt).

I believe so fervently in prayer and God's redemption. I know what He did in my life. I'm not under a bridge somewhere, but I could have been. I'm not in a drunken heap somewhere, but I could have been. I was broken, but God put me back together again.

A recent social media post caught my attention:

> My story is filled with bad choices. Broken pieces. And a lot of hurt. It's also filled with a major comeback. Freedom in my life. Peace in my soul. And a Savior that restored everything.

I thought, *That pretty much sums it up. Been there. Done that!* Life is full of decisions we'd like to take back and relationships we'd like to do over. People hurt us, and we hurt people. It's messy. We wonder, *Is this my lot in life? Is that all there is? A life of settling? Regretting?* We all want a level of happiness and peace, joy, and love. We crave relationships in which we can be real, raw, and accepted.

Broken people are often thrown away. We often throw ourselves away. We sense we are no longer useful for anything or to anyone. We feel as if we have passed our expiration date. With brokenness there is a sense of, *Does anyone see me? Hear me? Care about me?* We wonder, *God, where are You?*

I've had multiple times of feeling broken. Past my usefulness. Discarded emotionally. I needed help! There were seasons when I thought I'd hit rock bottom, but then I realized there was more. The bottom felt like discouragement. It felt like depression. I identified with Nehemiah, who was so forlorn that the king asked him, "Why does your face look so sad when you are not ill? This can be nothing but sadness of heart" (Nehemiah 2:2 NIV). I needed a conduit to the Holy Spirit.

This is where you and I come in! We have faith, hope, and love for those who are wandering. We know from our own experiences that there is a better life available, free for the taking. We can pray from a place of knowing that there is nothing too broken for God to put back together again. Let's pitch our tents (prayers) in the land of hope (see Acts 2:22–28 MSG).

Flying home one day, I was seated across from a man who appeared to be in physical distress. The flight crew was busy preparing for take-off, so, having been a flight attendant (or "stewardess" as I was called a very long time ago), I took matters into my own hands. Kind people around me rearranged seats, and I was able to put this man next to me. I learned he had walked out of a hospital injured. I asked if I could pray for him, and as I prayed, God showed me a broken heart—not just physically but also emotionally and spiritually. This man slept while I prayed and prayed some more. We arrived at my destination but not his. After arranging for ground and flight assistance to his destination, I slipped my business card into his pocket.

Years later I received a call at work. It was my mystery travel companion. He relayed a wonderful story of an upside-down, once-broken-but-now-put-back-together life! I had merely helped with what he needed in the natural, but God used a "ministering angel" (his words) to begin putting his life back together spiritually, emotionally, and physically. Only God! He used my little to do so much.

In Luke 24, after the crucifixion, two men were wandering on the road to Emmaus. There were not lost; they were walking dazed, trying to grasp all that had gone wrong. The resurrected Jesus joined them. They didn't recognize Him, though, and wouldn't until they sat at dinner and He broke the bread and blessed it. Then they recognized the very One who comes to our brokenness and blesses it. They recognized the Bread of life, the One who was broken and blessed for you and me—the Lord Jesus.

Let us pray with renewed purpose and passion! Father God is going to rescue His people. Jesus will leave the 99 and go after the one. He will recapture the hearts of the wounded and broken, in the church and outside its walls. He will call His Church, the Bride of Christ, back to all truth! He will rescue, heal, and put the broken pieces back together.

Let our prayers be the hand that reaches out for the hem of His garment.

Let our faith be the faith that moves mountains and casts them into the sea.

Let our hope be the anchor for those living in a sea of hopelessness.

Let our love be the balm that heals broken hearts.

Our prayers will move the heart and hand of God. It is never too late. Now is the time. Pray, saints!

15

SAY YES TO BETTER FLOUR

My much-anticipated purchase from a favorite baking website finally arrived. I was excited about what was in the box. However, what really caught my attention was the tape that sealed the box! It said, "Say Yes to Better Flour." Oh, this echoed what God was just talking to me about that very morning—my saying yes to more of Jesus, the Bread of Life, and being fed manna (better flour) in response to a current prayer assignment. Our praying life will always begin and end with Jesus and the Word. He is the *better flour! He is the Word!* These five little words underscore the heart of this book. Saying yes to the presence of God. Saying yes to cultivating a praying life that glorifies Him. Saying yes to His ways that are higher than mine. Saying yes to more of Jesus and the Word of God is always the answer!

The following verses are all about wheat, grain, harvest, flour, and all those wonderful words that echo showbread—the holy, consecrated bread ever present in the Tabernacle and Temple (and in our hearts) that represents God's continual presence and provision for us. You can only imagine how much joy I received when I found a special bread Scripture in the Old Testament. Buried among some hard-to-pronounce family names of the tribe of Judah, I saw "Jashubi-Lehem" (1 Chronicles 4:22). "Lehem" caught my attention because I knew it meant bread. Looking up this ancient man's name, I discovered it means **"Bread Returned"** and "Refreshed or restored by the Bread." I loved it so much that I asked my dear friend-like-a-brother Casey Cook to make me a rolling pin with *Jashubi-Lehem* inscribed in Hebrew.

"Returned" reminded me of a favorite Scripture in Ruth 1:6:

> Then she [Naomi] arose with her daughters-in-law that she might **return** from the country of Moab, for she had heard in the country of Moab that the **Lord had visited His people by giving them bread** (bold added).

God had visited His people by giving them His presence. Oh, that we would return to, be refreshed by, and receive the presence of God! Just writing this makes me want to go make challah. I love the book of Ruth. The references to bread, wheat, gleaning, and threshing floors (intercession) are so rich!

This next one was one of those how-do-You-do-this-God Scriptures. Many Christians know it by heart because they hear it quoted so often: "And we know that all things work together for good to those who love God, to those who are the called according to *His* purpose" (Romans 8:28). One day the Holy Spirit led me to dig a little deeper into the word purpose. The Greek is *prothesis,* meaning 'setting forth.' Four times in the New Testament, purpose refers to showbread—the bread of setting forth.

In Romans 8:28, *prothesis* means a deliberate plan, an intention, a design. In the Old Testament, the bread was "setting forth," continually fulfilling God's purpose to be ever-present with and make every provision for us. God's deliberate, forever plan was to set forth the living Bread—Jesus—so we can be set forth to fulfill His plans and purposes.

Dear ones, let us go forward into the plans and purposes of God, carrying His presence and representing Him wherever we go, in whatever we say, and to whomever we meet.

From the prayer chair to the courtyard.

From the Word written to the Word proclaimed.

From the whispered voice of God to the declared voice of His praying Church.

Being the bread baker I am, I loved finding Deuteronomy 28:5: "Blessed *shall be* your basket and your kneading bowl." Maybe that's why the Holy Spirit prompted me to pray while kneading!

What started this journey was, of course, Jesus. Doesn't everything perfect and good begin with Him? Begin with Bread!

> I am the bread of life (John 6:35).

> I am the living bread which came down from heaven. If anyone eats of this bread, he will live forever; and the bread that I shall give is My flesh, which I shall give for the life of the world (John 6:51).

Of the 20 times bread is mentioned in the Gospel of John, chapter 6 has 14 references. I encourage you to read that chapter out loud. Repeatedly. Over and over again. Listen to it on audiobook. Write it on the lampposts of your life and your heart. The Bread of Life was broken and blessed for you and me.

Now, Jesus isn't the only bread that came from heaven. God gave the Israelites manna to eat while they were in the wilderness for 40 years. I love the word *manna*. It literally means "bread from heaven." The apostle John writes in Revelation 2:17, "He who has an ear, let him hear what the Spirit says to the churches. To him who overcomes I will give some of the hidden manna to eat." Today, the Word of God is our daily bread! Our manna. Our bread from heaven.

Here's an interesting tidbit:

> It is impossible to know exactly how much manna came pouring through that portal during those 40 years, but one can make a rough estimate. If the Israelites numbered approximately 3,000,000 people, as many Bible scholars believe, it is estimated that they needed 4,500 tons of manna every day. If they gathered 4,500 tons a day every day for 40 years, that means an estimated 65,700,000 tons of manna supernaturally appeared on the ground over that period of time.[7]

That's a lot of bread! And it must have been very nourishing, for it sustained the people physically for all those years. Can you imagine the children who were raised in the wilderness, knowing nothing else? To them it was as expected as you and I going to a grocery store to buy a loaf of bread.

Here's some bread of heaven for you to research, enjoy, and get revelation from as you study the Word of God.

> And I will bring a morsel of bread, that you may refresh your hearts (Genesis 18:5).

Keep reading. Jewish sages speak of this meal as the first Shabbat!

---

7. Rick Renner, *Sparkling Gems From the Greek Volume 2: 365 New Gems To Equip And Empower You For Victory Every Day Of The Year* (Tulsa, OK: Institute Books, 2016, Kindle Edition).

You gave them bread from heaven for their hunger (Nehemiah 9:15).

Most assuredly, I say to you, unless a grain of wheat falls into the ground and dies, it remains alone; but if it dies, it produces much grain (John 12:24).

And bread *which* strengthens man's heart (Psalm 104:15).

He makes peace *in* your borders,
And fills you with the finest wheat (Psalm 147:14).

Blessed *is* he who shall eat bread in the kingdom of God! (Luke 14:15).

His winnowing fan *is* in His hand, and He will thoroughly clean out His threshing floor, and gather the wheat into His barn; but the chaff He will burn with unquenchable fire (Luke 3:17).

Then He said to them, "The harvest truly *is* great, but the laborers *are* few; therefore pray the Lord of the harvest to send out laborers into His harvest" (Luke 10:2).

Oh, I must stop now and leave you to your own journey through the Scriptures to be fed, nourished, sustained, strengthened, and blessed by the Word of God! Jesus is the Word, and Jesus is the Bread of Life.

He is risen!

Mark 16:6

16

SANCTIFIED NO

When we first say yes to Jesus, we are saying yes to a life that is no longer our own. That's right—the bill of sale belongs to Him. Bought. Paid for. No debt. "Yes" means we follow His lead. "Yes" means our talents and gifts are not buried but rather are on full display for God to be glorified. That singular yes initiates us to a life of full-time ministry.

In the excitement, honor, and eternal reward wrapped up in that "yes" is also a "no"—a sanctified no. "God's yes" means saying no to good things when He has called you to God-things. "God's yes" means saying no to pleasing man. And sometimes, "yes" means saying "no" to the needs of the church, family, friends, etc. What happens if you only say "yes" and never learn to say "no"?

Several years ago, I was in a season in which my cup didn't overflow. That's a nice way of putting it, really. My cup wasn't wet. It wasn't even damp. No, it was bone dry. I loved Jesus, loved His Church, and loved my ministry responsibilities, yet all that loving had landed me in my doctor's office. My body was telling me something my heart didn't want to hear.

My doctor listened to me, and then he listened to my body. As he pulled out his prescription pad, I silently thanked God that there was a solution and a remedy for everything that ailed me. Imagine my surprise when my doctor started drawing a picture. He drew a box that took up two-thirds of the page. Then he drew horizonal lines from side to side. With a final physician's flourish, he wrote, "Live within the margins." I thought, *What*?! No pill. No ointment. No diet changes. Nothing but good counsel. After much thought, I realized I was given a prescription for a sanctified *no*.

Later at home, with this prescription in hand, I sat in my prayer chair. I began asking God, "How? Why? What now?" I had so many (too many) commitments. My family needed me. People were depending on me. I loved finding joy and purpose in serving. Then guilt started setting in. The accuser started talking: "You're a failure. You're not strong enough, smart enough, or brave enough to serve. You're letting people down. God is counting on you. God gave you this desire, and now you're walking away. You can't keep up. You. You. You." He was relentless. I was left dealing with guilt, shame, confusion, sadness, and a deep weariness. Like Elijah, all I wanted to do was run and hide.

I had no choice. My body, my husband, my doctor, and the Spirit of God were saying, "Stop." In the name of love, stop! It was time to retreat and refocus. It was a real-life, "Come to me, all you who are weary and burdened, and I will give you rest" (Matthew 11:28 NIV) wakeup call.

Months later, our church hosted an evening of prayer to encourage volunteer intercessors. I didn't want to go. I had a long list of reasons—good ones—why not to go, but God compelled me to attend. Now, I'll admit that this compelling took more than a little nudging—it became a point of obedience. I arrived late enough to avoid talking to people, and I found a seat in the very back row, right next the exit.

Well into the meeting, the speaker randomly called on attendees to give them encouraging words. Wanting nothing more than to be invisible, I slipped into the ladies' restroom. "God, may I leave now? No one will notice." A resounding *no* sent me back to my anonymous seat. At least I thought it was anonymous. But then I heard, "Will the lady in the back row with the white top on please come forward?" I thought, *Lord, erase me. Hide me. Get me out of this*! Still, I walked forward.

The speaker prayed and thanked the Lord for me, asking for a time of refreshing in God's presence.

> There is a real healing that is going to take place in the spiritual. I pray over her, Lord, for the weariness to leave her right now, in Jesus' name. We remove the weariness of soul, the weariness of even fighting some of her own battles ....
>
> Mary Jo, you have felt kind of guilty because you have been AWOL. And the Lord comes to you tonight and says He has given you a leave of absence. You are no longer to carry that guilt. He didn't place it there. He didn't put it upon you. He sent me here to tell you that you are not AWOL—you just have a leave of absence with His permission.
>
> There were days you felt like you were led of the Holy Spirit, and you had a sense of being led of the Holy Spirit. But the last several months, you felt like you haven't been led; you feel like you're being driven. That sense of being driven is going to be broken.
>
> So I come in the name of Jesus, and I break this lying spirit off Mary Jo. You can no longer drive her; you can no longer take hope away from her, in Jesus' name. Hopelessness, we command you to loose her mind and to loose her thoughts. No more condemnation. No more sense of failure. No more hopelessness. No more living out of reserve.

> And now I release the joy of the Lord. I release the fountain of youth. That vitality. I restore even the strength to this physical body now. Body, hear the word of the Lord. Receive the strength of the Lord. Receive the joy to add strength to her, in Jesus' name.

Saints, your service to God, your lives of prayer and intercession, your earthly vessels … all of that *must* be stewarded wisely. God did not design us to live without margins or serve without boundaries. Otherwise, we find ourselves spouting out unsanctified yeses as we become more tired and burned out than we ever thought possible.

Commit only to God-directed assignments. Recognize that some appointments are for a specific season or reason and not necessarily a lifetime. Get your spouse or an accountability partner to weigh and measure your yeses. Welcome the seasons where God pulls you aside, because these times will indeed come. It's always better when the time-out is for refreshing instead of healing.

> Come to Me, all who are weary and burdened, and I will give you rest. Take My yoke upon you and learn from Me, for I am gentle and humble in heart, and YOU WILL FIND REST FOR YOUR SOULS. For My yoke is comfortable, and My burden is light (Matthew 11:28–30 NASB).

Lord, I confess I get in the way of serving You to my own detriment. Holy Spirit, thank You for conviction and not condemnation as I relearn how to live my life of serving and being. I know that joy from Hebrews 12:2 comes from only doing what the Father is asking me to do. Oh, for the wisdom to hear and obey! In Jesus' name, Amen.

17

SABBATH: A CALLING
The Church's Story

Church history during the late 1960s and early 1970s was marked by the Jesus Movement. As the Spirit of God moved across the United States, people and churches awakened to a fresh revelation of a personal relationship with Jesus. Accompanying this revelation was a swell in the making of prayer-disciples. Men and women, young and old, across denomination lines and outside the walls of the church were experiencing a deep desire to connect with God though worship and prayer. Christian bookstores opened with shelves full of books on the spiritual discipline of prayer. And this was not prayer in a religious box but rather grassroots, where-the-rubber-meets-the-road-of-life prayer. Catherine Marshall was a forerunning author of so many classics about how to connect and *stay* connected to God through illnesses (tuberculosis), deaths (early widowhood), blended families, and so much more. Yes, the Church was responding to the Spirit's call to relationship and partnership with God the Father, God the Son, and God the Holy Spirit.

Today I hear and see the same move of God regarding Sabbath. Is it in response to a Church filled with people who are tired, worn out, and over-volunteered? Marriages are hanging on by a thread (or not at all), families are scattered in all directions, and children are living in a world that challenges our faith, hope, and love of Jesus at every turn.

I'm not sure at this point about all the whys, but I am certain God is awakening His Church to His rest. His Sabbath. His holy day. Sermons are being preached, books are being written, and people are asking church leaders, counselors, and friends, "How do I find the right pace and rhythm to live? And not just live but also thrive with the joy and peace of the Lord?"

Often the Church looks more like a bridezilla than the bride of Christ. We are crawling down the aisle too tired for the wedding, let alone the marriage. This is not how we want to finish. God has a better plan for His bride. Read Romans 12:1–3 and think of this passage in terms of Sabbath-keeping:

> So here's what I want you to do, God helping you: Take your everyday, ordinary life—your sleeping, eating, going-to-work, and walking-around life—and place it before God as an offering. Embracing what God does for you is the best thing you can do for him. Don't become so well-adjusted to your culture that you fit into it without even thinking. Instead, fix your attention on God. You'll be changed from the inside out. Readily recognize what he wants from you, and quickly respond to it. Unlike the culture around you, always dragging you down to its level of immaturity, God brings the best out of you, develops well-formed maturity in you.
>
>   I'm speaking to you out of deep gratitude for all that God has given me (MSG).

What good counsel! We can learn from many who have found their way. First, we have so much to learn from our Jewish brethren on how to keep the Sabbath. A meal. An intentional, inviting rest into our home, our table, our family, and our day. We can learn from leaders who have gone before us and discovered the value, blessing, and necessity of Sabbath.

Traditions are such a part of Sabbath. One might also use the word *ethos*. Simply stated, ethos is the characteristic or spirit of a culture, era, or community demonstrated in its beliefs and aspirations. Ethos shares a root word with *ethics*. Personal ethos is your framework for making choices. Familial ethos is a validation of family values. Our churches, universities, and cities have certain values for which they are known—they usually list these in the "About Us" section on their websites. We determine and define what our ethos is and how it is lived out. Holiday traditions. Education. Sports. Honor. Family prayer time. Favorite recipes that show up on special occasions.

Is Sabbath truly a necessary part of our ethos? Yes, it is, on every level. In the natural, we have bodies, and like machines, we wear out. Emotionally, mentally, and spiritually speaking, we need tune-ups and updated parts, the most important of which is the heart. God's plan for His Church is to reflect the very best of Him, and that is rest, holiness, and wholeness.

Eugene Peterson was a pastor for 30-plus years, and he authored more than 30 books, including *The Message* Bible. On many occasions Eugene spoke of how he jumpstarted his spiritual life by keeping the Sabbath. That was the one deliberate thing he did that made the biggest difference to his family, his congregation, and himself. Given his pastoral responsibilities on the weekend, Eugene and his wife, Jan, chose Monday as their Sabbath. Their boundaries were defined by doing anything they wanted but nothing necessary. They would pray and play. Anything that fell in those two categories was allowed during this time of what he referred to as "spiritual rejuvenation."

In hindsight, Eugene said that Sabbath keeping was the most significant decision he and Jan made for his ministry. It was a choice that had to be made each and every week. Sometimes after hours of wrestling with the Lord about writing or making a call, the surrender would come: "Okay, Lord, I quit. It's your day."[8]

I've been involved in prayer and intercession for more than 45 years. I served 17-plus years on staff at a church that knew and loved ministry and people. I have experienced firsthand the pure joy of serving the church and others on my knees. But I can attest wholeheartedly that nothing can compare with the pure joy of Sabbath—the love, laughter, and engaging with God that culminates in Shabbat dinner and lingers till the next begins!

Oh, I wish I had learned these principles, this trust, and said yes to the whole of God's invitation earlier. I was late to the game, and I consequently suffered in my body, soul, and spirit. But that doesn't mean I can't learn from my mistakes. With all that is in me, I'm going to encourage others to learn and linger in the grace of Sabbath keeping.

We know worship is warfare. But saints, rest is warfare too. There's an old saying: "If the devil can't get you to sin, he can keep you busy." Busyness isn't always wrong—we all have busy seasons—but it can become sin.

Years ago, there was a group of intercessors involved in high-level spiritual warfare. The wounded and battle weary were taking so many of the enemy's hits. They regrouped and sought God on how to stand, resist, push back, and advance

---

8. Sandra Glahn, "Eugene Peterson: That 'Good-for-Nothing' Sabbath," Aspire2: Thinking That Transforms, March 13, 2015, http://aspire2.com/2005/06/eugene-peterson-that-good-for-nothing.

victoriously. The Spirit challenged them to observe the Sabbath. They took that counsel to heart, each person seeking God about how that would look like in their lives. Spread across various states, they committed as a group to begin keeping the Sabbath. They determined that one of their guidelines would be not to do anything that might keep others from keeping the Sabbath. This meant no shopping, dining out, etc. They planned meals and household work, and they chose to keep Sabbath together.

The resulting testimony was powerful! The warfare dramatically stopped. They were clearer in mind and strategy. Their unity increased as God spoke Scriptures and revelations to each one that linked them together as a whole. They were happier and healthier.

Yes, my dear ones, Sabbath is warfare. God's rest resists, pushes back, and defeats the enemy's plans to steal, kill, destroy, and throw us off our assignments.

I know Scripture only says to test God in one area—the tithe (see Malachi 3:8–10). May I humbly suggest that God is offering and inviting us to learn a new way to live, breathe, and flourish? A new way to encounter and enjoy His presence. A new way to get filled up so we can carry His presence with us wherever we go throughout the week. I challenge you not to test God but to give Him three months and see what He will do!

As a Church, we are followers before we become leaders. We are to follow Jesus Christ, the Lord of the Sabbath. Jesus did not put a yoke of law on His Sabbath keeping but rather the grace of God. He did what the Father said to do on the Sabbath and thereby honored it. Jesus healed on the Sabbath. He spent time with His disciples on the Sabbath. He honored the Sabbath.

How will the Church steward this commandment? What does that look like lived out? We must find the answer. There is way too much roadkill in God's family. We must take personal responsibility. We must be the ones who set God-ordained boundaries around our Sabbath. We must pray for our leaders who serve within the four walls of the church as well as out in the world.

Let me end this chapter by introducing you to the *Amidah*, referred to as "The Prayer." It literally means "standing" and is a series of blessings recited in a synagogue while people stand. On Sabbath there is an added special blessing:

> "Our God and God of our Father,
> Be pleased with our *rest*."

Saints, may God be pleased with your rest. Not your work. Not your projects. Not your kingdom work. Not your ministry. Rather, God be pleased with your rest. Isaiah 66:1 says,

> Heaven *is* My throne,
> And earth *is* My footstool.
> Where *is* the house that you will build Me?
> And where *is* the place of my rest?

Let Him look no further than to you and me—His Bride, His house of prayer.

I'm so proud of you. Of your willingness to break old molds of living. Of your desire for more of God. Of your passion for His best and His rest. A Church that wars and serves from a place of rest is a true reflection of our Lord of the Sabbath, Jesus Christ.

18

DESPERATE TIMES CALL FOR DESPERATE PRAYING

"Nooooooo! Praying now!" This was my immediate response to a message about my dear friend Alisa who was admitted to the hospital after struggling at home with COVID-19 for 10 days. Flooding my heart and soul were the names and faces of people I had been praying for during THE pandemic. Many tragic stories had been shared, many tears had been shed, and many desperate prayers had been prayed.

The first report was very encouraging. Alisa responded well to the hospital's treatments and medicines, and she was soon released to continue care at home. So you can imagine the shock when less than 24 hours later, she was taken back to the hospital, admitted to the ICU, and eventually transferred to a special COVID-19 floor for patients in critical condition.

The following day's report showed no improvement. "She is still in critical condition, but they have managed not to put her on a ventilator. That is still a possibility. It is serious." The ventilator was a major concern! Doctors reported concerns about organ damage and blood clots. And then came the report that she was put on a ventilator. Then taken off. Then put back on.

My spirit cried out, "Lord, help us pray!" And He did. During my listening and praying time with God that morning, I opened a 365-day devotional to a "random" (God-selected) day. The title was "Our Partner in Prayer."[9] Author Rick Renner broke down the meaning of a beloved, Holy Spirit Scripture:

> In the same way the Spirit [comes to us and] helps us in our weakness. We do not know what prayer to offer *or* how to offer it as we should, but the Spirit Himself [knows our need and at the right time] intercedes on our behalf with sighs *and* groanings too deep for words (Romans 8:26 AMP).

My heart quickened as he described my intercession these past days—from praying the absolute truths of the Word of God to finding Scriptures that built faith and hope to beseeching the Father without words. My tearful prayers had become wordless, desperate groanings.

Rick went on to describe the Greek meaning of the words in this Scripture:

- *Intercession* literally "conveys the idea of a rescue operation." The example given was someone who fell into some trap, and someone else (the Holy Spirit) quickly comes to the rescue and delivers them.
- *Groanings* mean deep inward sighs and could be translated "vent." The example Rick used to describe this response from the Holy Spirit is turning up the fire under a teapot until the water boils and begins to let steam out. *Vent.* Here is the Holy

---

9. Rick Renner, "Our Partner in Prayer," Renner Ministries, September 29, 2021, https://renner.org/article/our-partner-in-prayer/.

Spirit raising incredible, powerful, and miraculous prayers within our spirits—those anointed groaning prayers for which there are no words.

The Holy Spirit can intercede for and through you while you're grappling with your inadequacies in prayer.

The next update reported that Alisa had a downturn, and after she was on the ventilator all night, her doctors were struggling to bring her off it. I recalled my lingering, "Teach me how to pray" conversation with Holy Spirit, and I texted Alisa's friend, Bonnie: "I have a prayer strategy. Can we talk?"

I knew we wanted to declare *life* over Alisa's body! Remembering Jesus' three days in the tomb, I suggested Bonnie and I pray in the Spirit for three minutes and allow the Holy Spirit to *vent* for Alisa and get her off that ventilator. Then we would pray and declare any Scriptures, thoughts, or pictures that came to mind.

Pacing in my backyard with my phone on speaker, a symphony of prayers we did not understand came forth. We followed with faith and power-filled, Holy Spirit-led proclamations over Alisa's body. It was a full court press of prayers to strengthen Alisa *today*! We declared, "Fight, Alisa! Fight! God is with you!"

The very next day Alisa texted, "Doc feels like there is an improvement. Somewhat out of woods. Gonna be here at least two more weeks. But I'm gonna make it. I will survive!" Six days later, she was released from the hospital, and the Lord completed the good work and miraculous healing He had begun.

Here are some very important take-aways and prayer lessons:

- I did my part. We did our part. There was a multitude of family, friends, and church partners around the world praying for Alisa's healing. We added our prayers to theirs.
- There are biblical and scriptural principles for prayer and intercession, but there are no formulas. We sought the Lord on how to pray, and He gave us a specific strategy for this situation.

Another prayer need arose a couple of weeks later. This time someone I know posted a very urgent prayer request for their sister who was hospitalized and in critical condition with COVID-19. The Holy Spirit nudged me to contact this individual to pray with her. Although so many of the circumstances were similar, our first prayer was still, "Father, how do you want us to pray?" On speakerphone this woman, her husband, and I prayed for 10 or 15 minutes together. We prayed in the Spirit, and we prayed with understanding. Listening to what the Holy Spirit said to each of us, we came into agreement with Spirit-led prayers. I'm grateful to report that this young wife and mother is now home and slowly recovering.

We have entered a time in the church where praying (versus saying "I will pray for you") has been elevated and emphasized by God. He wants us to add our faith to one another. There is power when words come forth that agree with the Word of God and the will of God. These desperate prayers are underscored when we pray together. Romans 8:27 says it best: "Because the Spirit intercedes [before God] on behalf of God's people in accordance with God's will" (AMP).

We must not limit our prayer life or our ability to hear God by subscribing to a one-size-fits-all formula. "This is how it happened last time, so this is how it should happen this time."

It's imperative that we develop a personal, active, and living relationship with the Holy Spirit.

I write about prayer partnerships in another chapter. I'm so burdened when people don't have someone to pray with and to "carry one another's burdens." Physical, on-earth prayer partnerships are one of God's kindest gifts to us. But if you're without such a prayer partner, please don't despair—I want you to know that you have a prayer partner in God the Holy Spirit Himself.

Get to know the Holy Spirit who prays the perfect prayers for you! Know Him as Comforter and pray He brings comfort to people in desperate need. As the Spirit of wisdom, He brings godly wisdom to situations that are beyond our reasoning and understanding. Get to know the Holy Spirit as Teacher, Advocate, Counselor, and Friend.

We live in desperate times. We have desperate prayer needs—physical, spiritual, emotional, mental, relational, financial, and so on. These needs call for a prayer life anchored in the anointing of the Holy Spirit.

19

ALL-ACCESS KEYS

"Do you know where my keys are?" It's a familiar refrain, right? One time, my sister Bernadette lost her keys. For two days, she searched everywhere. Purse. Kitchen counter. Find-anything-bowl. Garage. Office. Car. Clothes. *Nothing*. On the third day, she prayed and left for work with her second set of keys. Arriving at her destination with her second set of keys in her right hand, Bernadette opened the back door to retrieve her briefcase. She looked at her left hand, and there was her original set of keys—in her hand! How? We don't know. All we know is she was holding two sets of keys, one set in each hand.

God never loses His keys. They're always available to us. They aren't usually physical keys but rather spiritual keys—His Word—for kingdom praying. In Matthew 16:19, Jesus says, "I will give you the keys of the kingdom of heaven" (ESV). Authority keys allow us to do kingdom business, to open and shut doors and bring God's plans and purposes on earth as it is in heaven.

> The **key** of the house of David
> I will lay on his shoulder;
> So he shall open, and no one shall shut;
> And he shall shut, and no one shall open (Isaiah 22:22, emphasis added).

My friends Christa and Marshall were praying for a firstborn. They already had two pre-born babies in heaven, and the heartache, grief, and fear hung like a heavy cloud lingering over there-is-still-hope prayers. One day, I was in the middle of a very unusual prayer assignment: "Do all eight prayer watches."[10] I was in the fifth prayer watch (6–9 am), which had an emphasis on a time of renewal of the soul and outpouring of the Spirit. That morning my prayers were centered on "the Sun of Righteousness will rise with healing in his wings" (Malachi 4:2 NLT). I began to pray for my friends and asked *Jehovah Rapha*, Jesus our Healer, to touch Christa's womb. Scriptures came to me: "He heals the brokenhearted" (Psalm 147:3 NLT) and "I am the Lord who heals you" (Exodus 15:26 NLT). I could sense a spirit of faith arise in me, the gift Paul writes about in 1 Corinthians 12:9.

I knelt and prayed by my listening chair. I ended up in Exodus 23, reading about the Feast of Unleavened Bread. "At the appointed time ... you came out of Egypt" (v. 15). Then tears splashed as I read on:

> You shall serve [only] the Lord your God, and He shall bless your bread and water. I will also remove sickness from among you. No one shall suffer miscarriage or be barren in your land; I will fulfill the number of your days (vv. 25–26 AMP).

This was a promise for Christa! No more miscarriages or barrenness. I looked up when the next Passover was—12 months away. I felt so deeply in my spirit that God was declaring my friend would have a baby by Passover.

---

10. A prayer watch is a three-hour period dedicated to prayer. For more information, I encourage you to visit: https://www.abbaheart.com/prayer-watches.

It was 7:30 am when I called Christa and asked her if we could pray. Please know, this was a first for me—prophesying the coming of a baby is nothing to take lightly! It took courage birthed from a knowing, a conviction, a revelation-and-prayer time. So with the keys of Scripture, I prayed and declared over Christa. As she held her womb, we spoke healing Scriptures. We joined in prayers of thanksgiving for her babies in heaven. We praised the Who of God and not the "do" of God. Then we left it in His hands. That was April 7. Maverick was born the following February 19! Before Passover. God fulfilled His promise!

Soon after, an acquaintance (now friend) was prompted by the Spirit to mail me a gift. It was a three-inch golden key with a note that read, "A key is to open and to close. We have spiritual authority to open, remove, and unplug forgotten wells, anointing rivers, and revivals. This key represents a power, authority, and trustworthiness. Isaiah 22:22. Love, Julie." It was good to be reminded! And it was so very timely because Christa ended up in the hospital fighting for her life. When Marshall called me, I grabbed my symbolic key, and we prayed and warred. Christa came home a few weeks later, and I'm happy to say mother, father, and baby are all thriving today.

There are several things I need to say. First, in no way, not even an ounce, do I believe that it was just *my* prayers that "worked." Oh no! There were multitudes praying for Christa and Marshall. I merely did my part to hear God, pray the Scriptures, and share as I was led with Christa for agreeing prayer. If I dared to put ownership on my prayers, I would give place to a root of pride. God spare me! While serving on our church staff over the prayer and intercession department, a value I put into practice with my leaders was nameless, faceless praying. May our names and faces be known in heaven, not with man.

Second, allow me to underscore how important it is that we are led by the Spirit in sharing the prayer-revelation God gives us. Ninety percent of what God tells me is kept between Him and me. Only 10 percent is ever spoken about outside my prayer room.

We have keys because God puts them in our hands. Like Bernadette's keys, they may appear to be lost, but God will speak and show us how to pray in His Word. God is reminding us of the authority He has given us! Like tumblers that fall into place, keys give us access to the will of the Father, the power of Jesus, and the work of the Spirit—all in God's perfect, appointed time.

20

CHALLAH-LUJAH HALLELUJAH

Travel back with me if you will, about 3,500 years ago. It's Friday, and the Israelites are preparing for the Sabbath. There's no record of the Sabbath being observed in Egypt, but here in the wandering wilderness, encamped around the Tabernacle of Moses, sunset is fast approaching. Soon God's honored and holy Sabbath rest will begin. And there is no worry about tomorrow, for He has provided a double portion of manna for Saturday's daily bread.

The sons of the Kohathites (from the tribe of Levi) are busy preparing the showbread (the bread of the Presence) to be set before the Lord continually (Leviticus 24:8). The priests prepare 12 fresh loaves following the recipe in Exodus 29:2, and then, with the solemnity of a worship service, the ceremony to exchange last week's loaves with the freshly baked showbread begins.

Twelve priests in ceremonial attire walk into the Tabernacle two by two, each carrying a fresh loaf of bread. The 12 loaves are to be placed in two rows separated by reeds to allow the air to circulate and the bread to stay fresh. At the table they solemnly begin the exchange. As one loaf is removed, the love offering of showbread is slipped into place. And the process is repeated until all 12 freshly baked loaves are in in place. I love imagining this holy exchange. It's so worshipful, intentional, and purposeful. It's so holy. I am tempted to take off my shoes as when God instructed Moses, "You are standing on holy ground" (see Exodus 3:5).

Fast forward thousands of years to our 21st century. It's Friday, and Jewish families all over the world are preparing challah bread for their Shabbat table. Bread, a staple of life from the beginning of time, links the old to the new to the now. Oh, it makes me pause and praise God for Jesus, our Bread of Life and our link from the old to the new to the now!

Now, it's time to join me in my kitchen, my second prayer room. Here the song "When Heaven Kissed Earth" speaks perfectly to my love of the Word of God about bread and the actual baking of bread, especially challah. What is it about challah that makes my heart sense the pleasure of God? Is it

- the making, kneading, rolling, and baking?
- the braiding?
- the fragrance?
- the golden appearance?
- praying over it and serving it to guests seated around the table?

If this were just a recipe, I would direct you to the appendix of this book or my YouTube demonstration.[11] But it has very little to do with a recipe or a technique. Rather, it has everything to do with the presence of God hovering over my kitchen like the cloud over the Tabernacle of Moses. Only God could turn a mundane-ordinary-routine chore into a bread-love offering.

---

11. "Begin with Bread – From the Pantry to Kitchen to Table," February 26, 2020, https://youtu.be/0Qj3nAKTV6M.

Remember, it is the bread of *His* presence, and it links us to the priests making the showbread thousands of years ago. As Jews and Gentiles come together to honor and observe the Sabbath, we come one step closer to the "one new man" vision Paul writes about in Ephesians 2:14–16. It's all so God-ordained!

A secret smile, a warm embrace, and an unexplainable joy come over me as I walk into the kitchen and begin setting up the tools and ingredients. Like little soldiers all lined up for duty, there is a growing anticipation of the things to come! Here in this sacred space, I mix flour, yeast, honey, salt, and a few other ingredients, only to discover new ways to hear God's voice, to feel His pleasure, and to create an offering. And all the while, the album *I Call You Friend* by Marty Goetz, my challah worship leader, plays in the background.

The practical aspects of making challah are interspersed with prayers. Some I wrote, and others I adapted from prayers I found in Jewish cookbooks or prayer books. Like a friend said to me, I once never thought of praying when I was cooking or baking. But now I do, and I love it! It elevates the why and the Who of our meals shared.

> My Lord God,
> Teach me to make Shabbat, sundown to stars up,
> an integral part of our relationship.
> Shape my heart to give and receive all
> that You've intended and desired
> for this holy day.
> I love You.
> Amen.

Before beginning the process of mixing and kneading, I pray a precious prayer I found in *A Jewish Woman's Prayer Book*. Perl, the wife of Rabbi Levi Yitzhak, prays with such a pure heart that she and husband will be like-minded, united in purpose, and that the work of their hands will be established.

> Master of the world: I ask of You—please help me, such that when my (insert your husband's name) recites the blessing over these loaves on Shabbat, he should have in his heart the same meditations that I have at this time, as I knead and bake.[12]

I add:

> May the pleasantness of the L-rd our G-d be upon us.
> Establish for us the work of our hands.
> Yes, establish the work of our hands (Psalm 90:17 MJP).

I love the following prayer. It demonstrates the heart behind this beloved mitzvah (law) of making challah and prayers from a relationship with God for you and your household.

> May it be Your will, our God and God of our forefathers, that the commandment of separating challah be regarded as having been fulfilled in all its details and requirements, and that the challah, which I now hold, be considered like the sacrifice offered upon the altar, which was accepted with favor. And just as in former times, the challah was given to the *kohen* [the priests] and that was an atonement for one's sins, so may it be an atonement for my sins, that I may be as one born anew, clean of transgression and sin, that I might fulfill the commandment of the holy Shabbat and these holy days, with my husband (and our children), to be nourished by the sanctity of these days. Through the commandment

---

12. Perl Yitzhak, "Perfect Unity," in *A Jewish Woman's Prayer Book,* ed. *Aliza Lavie* (New York: Spiegel & Graum, 2008), 192.

of challah may our children always be nourished from the hand of the Holy One, blessed be He, in His great mercy and kindness, and with great love, and may the commandment of challah be accepted as though I had given a tithe. And just as I hereby fulfill the commandment of challah with all my heart, so may the mercy of the Holy One, blessed be He, be aroused to protect me from sorrow and from suffering for all time. Amen.[13]

As I braid the dough, there is a growing awareness in my spirit that God is using this time to unite His chosen people and His Church, much like Perl's prayer that we would be like-minded and united in purpose and that the work of our hands would be established. The prayer for the atonement of sin, to be like a person reborn free of sin and transgression, reminds us that our Lord Jesus, our Bread of Life, was the perfect sacrifice who made atonement for us on the cross. He set us free from our sins and transgressions.

From the showbread in the Tabernacle of Moses to the aroma held dear by our Jewish brethren, to the challah bread in our kitchens, there is such a thread of the presence of God. The Church is awakening, and there is one new man coming! What a full circle!

This full circle is exactly what Jesus speaks of in John 6:50–51:

> This is the Bread that comes down out of heaven, so that one may eat of it and not die. I am the Living Bread that came down out of heaven. If anyone eats of this Bread [believes in Me, accepts Me as Savior], he will live forever. And the Bread that I will give for the life of the world is My flesh (body) (AMP).

---

13. "Prayer Upon Separating Challah," in *A Jewish Woman's Prayer Book*, 186.

Today we pray for revelation of this truth—this eternal, life-giving, Bread of Life truth!

> Lord, we pray that what has been shrouded in mystery would be revealed to Jew and Gentile alike—the revelation of Your broken and blessed body offered up for each of us. Amen.

May Jesus, our Bread of Life, be revealed in homes and hearts across this nation and around the world. Here is a prayer to invite the Bread of Life, Jesus into your life.

Lord Jesus, I acknowledge that living life my way separates me from You. I am so sorry and want to leave my sin-life to follow You. Your perfect love for me resulted in Your offering Your perfect life in exchange for my sin-life when You died on the cross. It is only in You, Your mercy and grace, that I am forgiven. You are the Bread of Life, and my heart belongs to You before all others. I fully trust You to lead me in this life. I now have eternal life with You. I will be eternally grateful. Amen.

From Challah-lujah to Hallelujah! Thank You, Jesus!

You gave them bread
from heaven for their hunger,
And brought water for them
out of a rock for their thirst,
And You told them to enter
and take possession of
The land that You swore
to give them.

Nehemiah 9:15 AMP

21

SABBATH: A COMMANDMENT
God's Story

> You are cordially invited
> to a weekly day of rest,
> Sabbath.
> I am requesting the
> pleasure of your company.
> Please RSVP.
> —God

The fourth commandment extends an invitation to every person for rest and holiness: "Remember the Sabbath day, to keep it holy" (Exodus 20:8; see also Deuteronomy 5:12). Now, why in the world would I call a commandment an invitation? Because like everything else God asks of us, free will is involved. Coupled with the commandment is an innate, divinely inspired desire to figure it out, live it out, and enjoy its blessings.

The spiritual practice of observing a weekly Sabbath may already be part of your life. You may find yourself in the category of "hit or miss," or you might be exploring the practicalities. Wherever you are currently, let's pause (a very Sabbath thing to do) and allow the Holy Spirit to set, reset, or refresh our Sabbaths.

VALUE

Sabbath shows us that we are valuable to God. It matters to Him when we live with shrunken hearts, fatigue, stress, and disconnection. It matters to Him that we trust Him with our time. So many of us work multiple jobs, care for sick or elderly loved ones, or do anything else you may fill in the blank. Listen, God cares. We matter to God. So much so that since the beginning of time He provided a day of rest (see Genesis 2:3).

INVITATION

Everything about Jesus is an invitation. New life. Healing. Mercy. Kindness. In Matthew 11:28, Jesus says, "Come to Me, all you who are weary and burdened, and I will give you rest" (NIV). Finding rest outside of Jesus is not rest; it's merely a reprieve from the craziness, busyness, distractions, overload, and burnout. Jesus is the Lord of the Sabbath (see Matthew 12:8). Time and time again, He offers us a grace-look at Sabbath through the lens of "I came to fulfill the law." Jesus made it clear that the Sabbath is to be a delight. The Hebrew word for delight means exquisite luxury and to be pampered. That's God's heart for our Sabbaths—*exquisite* (extremely beautiful) *luxury* (the state of great comfort and extravagant living) and *pampering*.

The Sabbath was created for man (you and me), not man for the Sabbath (see Mark 2:27). Take a deep breath. Breathe in the exquisite, luxurious love of God the Father, the rest of Jesus our Lord, and the wisdom of the Holy Spirit! And prepare to be pampered (indulged with every attention, comfort, and kindness; spoiled). I can't tell you what this will look like, feel like, or live like in your life. But what I can tell you is that this is God's heart for you. When we do our little, He will do His much!

REST

Why can we go on a vacation and come home tired? Why does a day of shopping, watching sports, or lingering naps refresh us for only a short time? The world offers one definition of rest, but God has another. Rest in God is being content in whatever state we find ourselves. Rest in God is a spiritual address from where you can live. And that rest begins with Sabbath practice and making the day holy.

DAY

God's commandment says a day—24 hours. Isn't that just like God? In a world where we say, "I don't have enough time," God says, "Give Me 24 hours, and I'll give you more time." It's almost a fish and loaves story. I give God my little, and He multiplies back to me so much. Unless you have already experienced this physical, mental, emotional, and spiritual blessing firsthand, then you are going to have to trust me and others who have. Giving God 24 hours of rest replenishes us fully, like only God can. It's like one day of Sabbath is better than a thousand elsewhere (see Psalm 84:10).

HOLY

"Be holy, for I am holy" (Leviticus 11:44 ESV) seems to be an unattainable goal. Holy in Scripture means separated from everything profane and defiled and dedicated to everything pure. Oh, dear ones, this is my prayer for you: "Blessed *are* the pure in heart, / For they shall see God" (Matthew 5:8). I pray that from living Sabbath, you will break through glass ceilings, brick walls, and religious boxes and get to know God better than you ever dreamed possible. This fourth commandment will be the door to so many answered prayers.

Sabbath has been referred to as a sacred space. I imagined Exodus 33:7–14 being a Sabbath conversation between God and Moses. Here Moses pitched a tent (Sabbath day) away from the busyness of camp (six-day week). There in the sacred, holy space, Moses met with God. The pillar of cloud (God's presence) rested at the tent's entrance (my kitchen where I bake bread, our table where we eat Shabbat dinner and fellowship, etc.). There Moses and God spoke face to face as friends (our desire). Then Moses left the tent (Sabbath) and reflected on the favor of God on his life. There is a desire for this Presence to linger and go with him back into that busyness of camp (life). God assures Moses, "My Presence will go with you, and I will give you rest" (v. 14 NIV).

Valued friends of God, this is our Sabbath: a day given to us by our holy God so that we can draw close to Him, honor Him, bless Him, and be so full of His rest that it goes with us throughout the week. I believe the Lord is saying this is our harvest season. You will sow rest and reap rest. You will sow holiness and reap holiness. You will sow time and reap time. He truly is your Lord of the Sabbath.

Dear God,

Yes. My RSVP is a resounding YES! Thank You, Lord, for this invitation and all that You have planned for us. This fourth commandment will be the door to so many answered prayers. In Jesus' name, Amen.

22

TREASURE HUNTING

During one of my rare visits back home to Michigan, my sister Bernadette literally dragged me to an end-of-the-rainbow shopping mecca, Treasure Mart. I'm certain this name came from the quote "One man's junk is another man's treasure." Treasure Mart was an old home converted into a time capsule. Every floor, every room, and every nook and cranny were filled to overflowing with yesterday's favorites: furniture, pictures, needlework, plates, vases, tablecloths, and an entire room of vintage kitchen supplies. Surrounded by a plethora of 50s and 60s memorabilia, I felt as if I had pressed rewind on my life. Books, records, maps ... you name it, they've got it. Fighting a sense of overload, my shopping instinct kicked in, and I became determined to find my fit-in-the-suitcase treasure.

Was it hours or just minutes? With Bernadette, it always seemed as if time flew by. We stopped so many times to laugh, tell stories, and guess "How much?" Shopping with my sister was an adventure. I didn't share the same joy of the hunt, but being with her brought back childhood memories of sharing life. I was loving every minute.

Then my eyes found my treasure: a lovely porcelain statue of a shepherdess holding wheat. She was a graceful, purposed, and peaceful reminder of some of the things I love most about Scripture (sheep, wheat, fields, Ruth, etc.), all wrapped up in one figurine. I'm not certain how much she cost. Five dollars, maybe? Or was it seven? It really doesn't matter now because this hidden gem has become a priceless treasure to me.

It wasn't long after our shopping expedition that Bernadette made an unannounced, unplanned, and unexpected move to heaven. Her precious heart just stopped beating. And now, 20 years later, my bisque porcelain lady has a very special place in my prayer room. She is a reminder of a gentler time, of laughter that filled my soul. My sister had convinced me that I had found the deal of the century, and I had to agree—Bernadette was the deal of the century!

Often the Bible can feel much like Treasure Mart. Hidden in those 66 books are 1,189 chapters containing 31,202 verses made up of 783,137 words (King James Version). They are filled with priceless treasures of wisdom, love, forgiveness, encouragement, direction, counsel, correction, and so much more! On those beloved pages, in the columns, footnotes, concordances, and scribbles on the sides, are personal notes highlighting faith, hope, and love. From cover to cover we find memories of conversations, promises, and dreams from yesterday, as well as promises, hopes, and dreams yet unfulfilled.

The proprietors of Treasure Mart knew my sister by name. Bernadette expertly navigated the 5,000-square-foot maze of rooms filled to overflowing. She knew just where to look for any category of stuff! And because she was familiar with the lay of the land, she was able to pinpoint an area or grouping she was hunting that day. She was intentional and determined not to leave without her "find."

Are you with me? That same intentionality, determination, and familiarity with the Scriptures is the answer to finding the treasures you're seeking, needing, and wanting. And as familiar as you may be with a chapter, verse, or story, God's Word is continually unfolding. He gives us wisdom and understanding in due season, enduring promises to undergird and strengthen us in valleys, and joyful words to celebrate those mountaintop encounters.

As I mentioned previously, one of my all-time favorite phrases in Scripture is from Exodus 33, when Moses pitched his tent away from the busyness of camp with the intent to meet with God. It's in this place that the glory cloud (manifest presence of God) rested, God referred to Moses as "friend," and God promised to go with him and give him rest! This place was called the *tent of meeting*. I have spent years meditating on those verses, living them, teaching them, and writing about them. After all, I am a tentologist!

Not long ago, I was reading Habakkuk 2:3:

> For the vision *is* yet for an appointed time;
> But at the end it will speak, and it will not lie.
> Though it tarries, wait for it;
> Because it will surely come,
> It will not tarry.

The phrase "appointed time" jumped out at me. Curious (often the Holy Spirit's prompting), I looked up the Hebrew word for it. Are you ready?

Moed: appointed place, appointed meeting, appointed time, tent of meeting.

There it was: "tent of meeting"! I closed my Bible and said aloud, "How do You do that?" God was adding to my conversation about meeting with Him and calling it an "appointed time"!

How does God take the inspired, inerrant, and infallible written Word and write on our hearts? It's pure joy! His confirming voice through the Scriptures speaks to us like no human ever could.

Your Bible is an eternal treasure. Here are some tips that will open the lines of communication between you and the Scriptures.

1. Pray Out Loud

This accomplishes so many things. First, you will get used to hearing your own voice praying. Second, as you listen to your prayers, you'll begin to recognize when they shift from what you're praying from your soul (mind, will, and emotions) to what the Holy Spirit is praying through you. There will be a flow, a spontaneity, and an awareness that you're praying what Father would have you pray. You'll have the thought, *Where did that come from*? It's the Spirit activating the Word of God in and through you. That's when you go to the Scriptures and do a word search using a Bible program or the concordance in the back of your Bible. Read through these Scriptures until one of them resonates deeply with you.

Third, and this is a bonus, praying out loud makes you much more comfortable praying in a group or with someone. By then, you're already used to the sound of your own voice!

2. Take Notes

When you're reading your Bible, take note of words, phrases, or stories that begin to resonate in your spirit. Can you see yourself in that story? Can you see the Scriptures pulling you into a godly principle? Can you hear the voice of God making application to the situations and circumstances of your life?

3. Journal

As the Holy Spirit opens Scripture for conversation, journal any words and impressions you receive. Also, journal your response to what God is saying. This allows you to process at a different, deeper level the voice of God, the application of His Word, and the ways Scripture personally relates to you.

Father, I know there are treasures hidden in Your Word just for me. These treasures will unlock questions I have and will bring forth healing in my heart, both spiritually and perhaps even physically. There are mysteries You want to tell me to transform my life, renew my mind, and be a personal love letter from You to me. Be with me, Holy Spirit, as I go on this treasure hunting journey with the Word. Walk me into the Scriptures. In Jesus' name, Amen.

23

TRIM THE WICK

There was a growing restlessness in my spirit, an increasing awareness that life as we've known it was over. My holy dissatisfaction mirrored the unholy unrest swirling around our nation like a tornado. In addition to the life-altering pandemic that had the medical community in crisis mode, there was racial and social turmoil accompanied by unprecedented violence in our streets, unparalleled political vitriol, introduction of new terminology that labels and categorizes people groups, and a "cancel culture" as the media attempted to control conversations. We were living a world turned upside down.

I was standing in my utility room washing groceries (the newest guidelines to staying healthy), and I asked myself, *What is one to do?* Although much of the angst had to do with how to respond in the natural, the internal gnawing I was experiencing had everything to do with how to respond in prayer. Hearing how Father wanted me to pray was drowned out with processing the realities we were all dealing with every day.

Frustrated, I retreated to my prayer room. Enough was enough! I must get heaven's perspective. My Bible on my lap, my journal open, and my pen in hand, I cried out, "Lord, teach me to pray" (see Luke 11:1). I waited. I listened. The Holy Spirit began ministering to my fears, anxieties, and concerns. It took some time, but God's peace did come. There was a comforting sense of His presence, and I felt a little like David who had learned to be strengthened in the Lord (see 1 Samuel 30:6).

Then the Holy Spirit led me to Matthew 25. Oh, that beloved picture of the five wise virgins who had enough oil for their lamps. This spoke to my desire that my prayer life would have enough oil (Holy Spirit) and be a bright light in this dark time. I continued reading, and my attention was drawn to the word *trimmed*.

> And at midnight a cry was *heard:* 'Behold, the bridegroom is coming; go out to meet him!' Then all those virgins arose and **trimmed** their lamps (vv. 6–7, bold added).

I looked that word up, and it literally means to *put in order.* My heart heard,

> "Mary, what worked in the past (in your prayer life)
> will not take you where you need to be
> moving forward."

I started breaking down Matthew 25:1–13 as an answer to my prayer.

- "The **wise** took oil in their vessels with their lamps" (v. 4). Let us be prepared to pray and partner with God in this unprecedented time in world and church history. May we have wisdom for these times.
- "The wise took **oil** in their vessels with their lamps" (v. 4). In addition to referring to the anointing of the Holy Spirit, oil symbolizes preparedness. God wants to prepare us! Our hearts are set on the Bridegroom coming to claim us and the

revival that will precede the greatest move of God this world has ever seen. Oh, to be prepared, saints!
- "Then all those virgins **arose** and trimmed their lamps" (v. 7). This is hardly the time to retreat and hide our light under a bushel. No, we must arise! Our light, our prayers, and our partnership with God and others will shine bright, and Jesus' name will be lifted up!
- "Then all those virgins arose and **trimmed** their lamps" (v. 7). Trimming in the Greek means 'setting things in order.' The Holy Spirit was emphasizing setting my prayer life in order!

"Trim my prayer life? Lord, what would that look like?" God was creating within me a holy dissatisfaction in my prayer life. I began asking questions:

- What needed to be trimmed (set in order) so my prayer life would have God's anointing for this season?
- What areas of my life of prayer could be brighter, stronger, and more anointed after putting it under the Holy Spirit's microscope?
- What are the strengths and weaknesses of my relationship and partnership with God?

I heard of someone who burned candles almost non-stop in her small apartment. She did not trim the wick. A couple months later, she noticed something black in the corners of the ceilings. She thought it was mold. A mold specialist came to examine the damage, only to report it was not mold. It was soot. That's right, soot! This woman's untrimmed candle wicks produced this black residue. If only she had known that trimming the wicks on your candles causes them to burn clearer and last longer!

After hearing this story, I realized that trimming the wick is the perfect prescription for a vibrant, light-bearing, and Holy

Spirit-led prayer life. I was all in! I dedicated the next 10 days for the Holy Spirit to highlight areas, and boy, was I in for some big surprises! (Read the next chapter to find out what those surprises were.)

Dear ones, it's time to trim our lamps and make certain that we have a ready supply of oil. I pray for you a fresh filling of oil—the Spirit of God—to prepare us for the days at hand and the days to come.

> Every branch in me that does not bear fruit he takes away, and every branch that does bear fruit he prunes, that it may bear more fruit (John 15:2 ESV).

Father, Jesus, and Holy Spirit: my heart resonates with what You are saying and what You are desiring of me. I know it's time! With a joyful heart, I willingly submit every aspect of my prayer life to You. Body, soul, and spirit, I welcome the course correction, the pruning, and the trimming for Your glory. In Jesus' name, Amen.

24

JUST KEEP TRIMMING

> Arise, shine, for your light has broken through!
>   The Eternal One's brilliance has dawned upon you.
> *See truly;* look *carefully*—darkness blankets the earth;
>   people all over are cloaked in darkness.
> But God will rise *and shine* on you;
>   the Eternal's bright glory will shine on you, *a light for all to see.*
>
> —Isaiah 60:1–2 (VOICE)

I hope you took time to slowly breathe in Isaiah 60:1–2. This, dear reader, is what God is preparing to do in you, on you, and through you. This is an exciting time to be pursuing a life of prayer. It is breakthrough time for us, our loved ones, the Bride of Christ, and our nation.

I have a high level of expectation and anticipation as I write this chapter. As we submit our prayer lives to the microscope of the Holy Spirit, we enter into a time of pruning. This is a process of submitting to the work of the Holy Spirit in our lives and committing to what He comes alongside us to do. In cooperating with the Holy Spirit, we are permitted and released to be a conduit of His power.

A life of prayer involves all of who we are. Body. Soul (mind, will, and emotions). Spirit. All three affect who we are in prayer, how we pray, how effective we are in prayer, how we hear God, etc. We are a three-in-one package deal! All three need our attention!

The idea of trimming (setting in order) the wick of our prayer life and putting it under the Holy Spirit's microscope is that strengths can be made stronger. Weaknesses can be minimized and replaced with strengths.

I dedicated 10 days for the Holy Spirit to highlight the areas of my life on which He would like me to focus. Some areas I have already mentioned in other chapters (such as "I Lay Claim to Your Evenings"), but others I will address here.

BODY

Does taking care of yourself fall way down on the list of your priorities? Do you need to see a doctor? Follow up on some medical advice? Eat better? Exercise more? Get more sleep? When the Holy Spirit asked me those questions, the only thing I could say in reply was, "Ouch!" My spirit is willing, but my flesh is tired and weak.

If this is an area the Holy Spirit highlights for you, you can trust that help is on the way! Don't be hard on yourself, and don't be afraid. God wants this for you! Let me pray.

> Father, Your Scriptures are full of healing, wholeness, and strength to run the race. Often our bodies hold us back. Please give us the strength and courage to face this head on. Lord, give us the wisdom we need to set this part our of life in order. Whether a baby step or huge leap, show us the way to go! We trust, Lord, that You are part of this trimming the

wick. We want our bodies to be a living, healthy, and whole offering to You. Amen.

I am mindful that there may be many reading this chapter who are fighting battles with their body that have nothing to do with taking care of themselves. It has everything to do with a diagnosis or disease. To you I speak peace. The way you battle glorifies God. Your faith glorifies God. You are living prayer!

SOUL

Lighten Up

For our light to shine brighter, we may need to lighten up! Carrying "unrighteous burdens" (the weight of the world, loved ones, etc.) on our shoulders must cease. There is a real art in leaving our burdens with God and trusting that He is walking with us and even going before us.

Of course, there are literal ways to lighten up, too. I have a friend who just makes me laugh! We need a good dose of laughter to balance our lives. When I put my apron on and make some bread, it brings me joy. Do you have a creative outlet that you have put on the shelf, something that brings joy to your soul? Perhaps God is saying to pick it up, dust it off, and let your creativity flow.

Prayer Partnerships

It is time to strengthen our where-two-or-more-are-gathered prayer relationships. If you don't have an active prayer partner, start by asking God to bring you one. Mutual, agreeing-prayer partners do not merely give human advice or opinions; no, they truly seek God on behalf of one another.

If you have a prayer partner already, is God asking you to do anything different? Do you need to talk less and pray more?

Plan Time

When discussing this "trim the wick" exercise, my friend Pastor Marcus Brecheen told me that the parable of the wise virgins in Matthew 25 teaches us that our relationship with God ultimately comes down to how we spend our time. It's all about priorities. Again, *ouch!* I'll leave that up to the Holy Spirit to expound on what your personal priorities need to be.

Home

When God impressed the need to get my "home" in order, I thought He was referring to my utility room. But for Bruce and me, getting our home in order meant updating our wills and purchasing burial plots and memorial stones. I know that might sound morbid, but honestly, it's the responsible thing to do for people our age. By the way, God did let me declutter my utility room and garage. Organizing is a real mental and prayer health boost!

SPIRIT

How can your relationship with the Word shine brighter? I've always wanted to write the Word of God out, from Genesis to Revelation, in calligraphy. Does God want to trim your meditating on the Word? Does He want you to read a chapter repeatedly or share Scripture with others? I know a young, engaged couple who committed to reading the book of Romans—all 16 chapters—out loud together every day for 30 days. Wow!

Words

Are your words measured, meaningful, and reflecting the spirit of God in you? A critical (opinionated) spirit is kryptonite to one's prayer life. In 2002, I was challenged to a 40-Day Murmuring and Complaining fast. I thought, *Me? My number one strength is positivity, and my number one spiritual gift is exhortation. I can't see where murmuring and complaining even fit it.* The truth is, murmuring and complaining *don't* fit in, though we are tested at every turn. In this world of social media, everyone has an opinion and a piece of advice. It's never been more important to filter incoming and outgoing words!

Sabbath

God challenged me that even though I write about Sabbath and teach about Sabbath and live Sabbath, there were still areas in my practicing Sabbath that needed to be trimmed. Now, no book is supposed to come with a guarantee, but rest assured—Sabbath rest is key! Living prayer at God's pace and rhythm is a powerful weapon of warfare.

Here are some other setting-in-order steps that come to mind:

- Pinpoint obedience.
- Take a class.
- Read a book.
- Be mentored.
- Mentor someone else.
- Steward finances.
- Sow seeds of kindness.

There is no limit to what or how God will speak to you. Be Holy Spirit creative!

This devotional came the very day God started this setting-in-order conversation:

> February 6, 2021. It is time to set some things in order. There are things to be given away, thrown away, and some rearranged. I know you are looking forward to having it done, not so much as doing it. But doing it will be therapeutic. Your mind can be more at rest when things are in order. Chaos often causes frustration. Items are hard to find when you need them. I bring order out of chaos. Follow My lead.
>
> Genesis 1:1–4 (NIV) "In the beginning God created the heavens and the earth. Now the earth was formless and empty, darkness was over the surface of the deep, and the Spirit of God was hovering over the waters. And God said, "Let there be light," and there was light. God saw that the light was good, and he separated the light from the darkness."[14]

After 10 days, I was armed with 10 object lessons, and I made a 30-day chart with three columns. I listed 10 items in each column. Each morning I laid them before the Lord and considered how each might look in my life that day. Each evening I would check the list. Not every point was made for every day, but each added to a new order to my life. I was spiritually and naturally setting things in order.

God is a God of order. He is teaming up with us to bring new anointings to our prayer life. As you trim your prayer wick, I declare Zechariah 4:7: "Grace, grace to it"—grace to every

---

14. Ras Robinson and Bev Robinson, "What the Lord Is Saying Today - February 2021," His Kingdom Prophecy, February 27, 2021, https://www.hiskingdomprophecy.com/what-the-lord-is-saying-today-february-2021/.

mountain that stands in the way of you pursuing the absolute very best that God has prepared for you. And for those areas in your prayer life that need trimming but will require a breakthrough, I pray Deuteronomy 2:3: "You have made your way around this hill country long enough; now turn north" (NIV). It's our time to shine our light with the oil of the Spirit!

25

PRISONERS OF HOPE

My heart was broken—not in the physical sense but rather in the deepest part of my emotions. Hooked up to an EKG, I lay on a flat bed, staring at the monitor. I could see my heart. I observed blood pumping through the arteries, each beat in perfect rhythm. I asked the nurse, "Can you see where it is broken?" She assured me everything looked perfect. I told her, "It's broken. You may not be able to see it. But I can feel it."

My younger sister had moved to heaven. Unannounced. Suddenly. Without notice. And as I said during her memorial celebration, "By biblical standards, her death was untimely, and her life was cut short. So many of us here today were not yet finished *living* with Bernadette."

I was caught off guard that a loss in the natural could literally make a heart, an organ, a part of the body, hurt. But it did. It ached. It had a dull beat to it. There was a pain like the piercing of an arrow.

Whether we experience the loss of a spouse, parent, sibling, child, unborn baby, or friend, the pain sends shock waves through us—body, soul, and spirit. We are left with questions that can only be answered by God.

Recently, a dear friend received that dreaded 3 am phone call: "There has been a terrible accident." Kathy's husband, Bob, had tragically died in a home gas explosion.[15] Now Kathy and their four precious daughters, along with their families, are living a chapter of their life they would not have written, each looking for the beauty in ashes (see Isaiah 61:3) Although there is much to be grateful for—11 family members left the house just hours before the explosion—there are broken hearts and broken pieces to put back together to move forward in their new reality.

And you, dear readers, have walked or know those who have walked through the valley of the shadow of death. "O Death, where is your sting?" (1 Corinthians 15:55). The reality is that there is a sting! Yes, we know heaven is real, God is good, and Jesus defeated death, but for now, there are broken hearts that desperately need a touch, healing, and peace.

Not long ago, two married international worship leaders were hit by COVID-19. Steven, the husband, was soon taken to the hospital. Isolated from his wife, Renate, and their children, with only phone calls for prayers and comfort, he eventually slipped from his earthly body into the presence of God. I reached out to Renate, and as we mourned together, I asked her, "Where was God?" She replied,

> That is a great question! I often wonder how this all works in the darkest times ... it's a mystery. I think God finds me. My bones melted within me when Steven passed. God found me right there. What I knew about God before, I still know today. It's been and is being tested but it stands. I have no doubts about God's goodness! I just miss my man terribly. My prayers are short and usually in the shower where the water

---

15. Natural gas detectors are easy to install, and they save lives. Bruce and I installed one right after the loss of our friend.

joins my tears. I have never felt God this close! Intimate. Yet I am heartbroken. The two are not mutually exclusive, I am finding out.

Renate told me that what gives her hope is seeing that she still has something to give—that even in her lowest moments God would use her to encourage someone.

On Easter, I sang "Worthy Is the Lamb" with my hands lifted high. And I meant it. That apparently touched people on a deep level because of my story. That gives me hope. That He still uses someone like me to carry His victorious story.

I asked the Lord why He wanted me to write this chapter. He answered immediately with one word: "Hope." I instantly thought of Zechariah 9:12: "Return to your fortress, you prisoners of hope" (NIV). *Prisoners of hope.* Hope to those wondering if they can draw a next breath. Hope to those walking through a valley of unanswered prayers.

There is much we can do in the natural to help our hurting loved ones. We can bring meals, run errands, return phone calls, and help with mountains of paperwork. But the question remains: *God, what can we do to bring Your hope?* Hope that, like the balm of Gilead, brings refreshment to a parched, dry heart. Hope that brings the comforting and healing Holy Spirit. Let's draw from the wisdom of *shiva*, the Jewish tradition for mourning. This set-apart period of seven days is a designated time to be with family and friends who have lost a loved one.

According to Jewish law, there is a specific etiquette for paying a shiva visit. Visitors are to enter quietly, take a seat near the mourner, and say nothing until the mourner addresses them first. This has less to do with ritual than with common sense: The visitor cannot know what the mourner most needs at that moment. For example, the visitor might feel that he or she must speak about the deceased, but the mourner might feel too emotionally overwrought to do so. Conversely, the visitor might try to cheer the mourner by speaking of a sports event or some other irrelevancy at just the moment when the mourner's deepest need is to speak of the dead. And, of course, the mourner might just wish to sit quietly and say nothing at all.[16]

Being there is enough. One's presence brings comfort as the grief is shared.

Through silent prayers, listening prayers, and waiting prayers, God will direct our words and actions. My friend Casey's wife, Amy, was a wonderful, faith-filled woman. Her love of Scripture and how she shared her revelations caused multitudes to drop anchor in faith, hope, and love. When her life was cut short, it was not from lack of prayer or fasting! She was surrounded by family and friends who warred for her healing with her. Shortly after Amy moved to heaven, Casey returned to work. A colleague looked at him with deep compassion, hugged him, and then walked away. That silent prayer said so much. No words were needed to convey the shared sorrow.

Listening allows us to hear what our loved ones are experiencing or feeling. How freeing is it to know that we don't have to have the right words or wisdom words or any words? The art of listening allows the Holy Spirit to direct our response, even if it is no response, and to guide our prayers moving forward.

---

16. Joseph Telushkin, *Jewish Literacy: The Most Important Things to Know about the Jewish Religion, Its People, and Its History* (New York: William Morrow, 2008), 705.

Isaiah 40:31 speaks of "those who wait on the Lord." As we wait and pray, God will show us how to be His conduits of healing to broken hearts. Be responsive to those Holy Spirit nudges. A picture. A memory. A note. A meal. A hug. A prayer. God will surely use our hope to remind them of Jeremiah 29:11: "'For I know the plans I have for you,' declares the Lord, 'plans to prosper you and not to harm you, plans to give you hope and a future'" (NIV).

While writing this chapter, I went to a Bible website to check on a reference. There on the landing page was the Scripture for the day:

> O DEATH, WHERE IS YOUR VICTORY? O DEATH, WHERE IS YOUR STING? ... Thanks be to God, who gives us the victory [as conquerors] through our Lord Jesus Christ (1 Corinthians 15:55, 57 AMP).

There is no question that God is speaking to us and encouraging us. We are learning not only how to walk through the valley of the shadow of death but also how to walk with others. Saints, we carry the presence of God. We carry His love, His sweetness, His compassion, and His kindness. And through our prayers, whether silent, listening, or waiting, God is going to use us to mourn with those who mourn and to bring hope to the hopeless.

But I would feed you
with the finest bread
and with the best honey
until you were full.

Psalm 81:16 CEV

26

MANTLED FOR HIS SERVICE
Submitted. Committed. Permitted.

> "Bring the mantle that is on you, and hold it." She held it; and he measured six measures of barley, and laid it on her.
>
> —Ruth 3:15 (World English Bible)

As I begin writing this chapter, a worship song titled "I Surrender All" begins playing in the background. How perfect. God sings over us as we pause to consider and pray about the mantle He has placed on you and me. In Scripture, a mantle refers to a gifting, a calling, a God-ordained-and-anointed purpose. Our gifting. Our calling. Our ordained-anointed purpose.

When considering a biblical example of picking up a mantle, we often think of Elijah and Elisha (see 1 Kings 19:19; 2 Kings 2:13). Many anointings (mantles) of God are passed from one person to another. Take Freda Lindsay as a modern-day example. She inherited the responsibilities and stewardship of Christ for the Nations Institute (CFNI) when her husband, Gordon, passed away suddenly.

Charged by the Board of Directors to pick up Gordon's mantle, there was no question of "Why me?" Instead, Mom Lindsay, as she was affectionately called, obeyed God's calling and took up her husband's mantle to oversee the physical and spiritual growth of CFNI.

Mom Lindsay didn't write her story—she lived the one God gave her. CFNI was established in Oak Cliff, a low-income neighborhood just south of downtown Dallas, Texas. In Scripture, Nathanael asked, "Can any good thing come out of Nazareth?" (John 1:46 WEB). The disciple might have asked the same thing about Oak Cliff. This neighborhood was neglected and left in ruins. But Mom Lindsey was not limited to what she saw or others said; she focused on the mantle God had placed on her to create an equipping school to plant churches and disciple nations. Mom Lindsey took CFNI from a single piece of land to a campus of more than 88 acres. When she passed away, there were more than 33,000 alumni, including thousands of international students from 108 countries. She had seen the expansion of CFNI with 48 associated Bible schools in 33 countries.

A few months before Mom Lindsay transitioned from this life to the next, Bruce and I were invited, along with several other people, to attend a special lunch with her. It was an easy yes! I was looking forward to seeing her again, and we had a delightful lunch. I could listen forever to her stories of the remarkable, miraculous ways God used her submitted, committed, and permitted life. We spoke of what God is doing now and touched on His plans for the future.

As we were leaving, a friend and I asked Mom Lindsay if she would pray for us. There in the grand hotel lobby, we knelt beside her as she laid hands on us. She prayed that we would be strengthened for the service of the Lord. She prayed that no weapon formed against us would prosper. She prayed an impartation of service for the kingdom. Even now recalling this holy moment brings tears to my eyes. It leaves me pondering the weightiness of what she said, the anointing she carried, and what God was saying to me through her.

After Mom Lindsay moved to heaven, I attended her celebration of life service. At the gathering, friends, family, and colleagues spoke about her incredible life achievements and the influences she had in biblical education, equipping the saints, worship, prayer and intercession, church planting, and Israel. It was astonishing to hear!

One speaker addressed Mom Lindsay's mantles. It was quite clear she carried more than one. This speaker challenged those attending and listening from around the world to inquire of the Lord what portion of her mantle God was anointing them to carry on! I remembered Mom Lindsay laying her hands on me and receiving an impartation from her. God whispered, "Prayer, intercession, and Israel." Yes, we shared a mutual love for all three! Years later, I led a prayer and intercession team to Israel. At the end of our 12 days, one of the members said, "You remind me of Mom Lindsay." This is only through the grace of God!

What is your mantle? All of us have a gift. It's just a matter of picking it up and wearing it with confidence, knowing God will supply all we need to carry it and serve Him and others.

Our God does not send us into any assignment without fully equipping us. I love the Scripture from Ruth 3:15. Kinsman-redeemer Boaz invited Ruth to bring her mantle (her cloak) and hold it before him. He then measured out six measures of wheat, which was an abundant, overflowing amount. What provision!

God loves to provide all we need to complete the purpose for which He has called us.

It wasn't long ago that I was sitting in my listening chair and pondering the holding pattern my life was in at that moment. Circling, circling, circling. Like airplanes waiting for clouds to open so they can execute a landing, I too was waiting to bring the way-too-long assignment that I knew was my mantle to completion (a landing).

The Lord reminded me of an assignment my teacher-turned-friend Cindy Jacobs had given me years before: write your calling. I pulled up the document on my phone and began reading it. Suddenly, the phone rang—it was Cindy! Twenty years had passed since I was in her class at Wagner (more on that in chapter 37), but in one of those God-suddenlies, we found ourselves seated at lunch within the hour, Cindy asked, "How is it going?" She sounded like the Holy Spirit. I knew exactly what she was referring to, and I gave her one of those "It's fine" answers that really means "Nothing is happening." Cindy looked at me like only Cindy can, pointed her finger, and said, "Get it done. *Now*. God called you to do this. It's time to get it done." After lunch, I came home and put my hand to the plow (computer). Nine days later I pressed send on my long-held assignment!

Sometimes it takes a Holy Spirit nudge through a memorial service or a friend to have your life circumstances rearranged and find that God is asking you for your mantle so He can fill it to overflowing with all you need!

I have labored, prayed, wrestled, and inquired of the Lord for months about why I was supposed to write this chapter for you. There's a strong sensing in my spirit that there are mantles and giftings that are ready and needing to be picked up. Whether you immediately obey like Mom Lindsay or struggle with a year of delay as I did, God is sounding the call! Do you hear it? Do you see it? Do you feel it? It's time to go deeper into your assignment. There are new fields and territories to be taken.

Years ago, my friend and singer-songwriter Mark Harris and I led a prayer-worship team through Israel. There in Bethlehem, Mark began singing a popular song he co-wrote, titled "What a Strange Way to Save the World." From the point of view of Jesus' earthly father, Joseph, the lyrics speak precisely to what we are talking about today. *Why me?*

I asked Mark about the song. This is what he told me:

> Like Joseph, we may grapple with wondering if we are capable of doing what God has asked us to do. So many times in this life we wonder, *God, why did You choose me to do what You're calling me to do? I don't feel capable.* Ultimately, we must trust Him enough to know that even though we may not understand, we'll do what He asks us to do. God's ways are higher and bigger than our ways.

I feel a surge of excitement for you, dear reader. God is ready to mantle you. Let me leave you with this encouraging devotional by Ras Robinson:

> God has released a trail blazer mantle upon you. With that mantle is an anointing impartation. You are gifted to make new trails leading to countless blessings for faithful followers. The Lord has placed along His trail for you markings and indicators for your sure guidance to his intended destinations. God desires that you consider your calling. Are you carrying out His instructions or have you stopped far short? Go back and recall and relive His words

of calling to you. No shame needed. But quick obedience is now required.[17]

> When I took a long, careful look at your ways, I got my feet back on the trail you blazed (Psalm 119:59 MSG).

Let us be like Ruth and lay our mantles before the Lord. He will fill them with every gifting, anointing, and calling we need to do what He has entrusted us to do!

---

17. Ras Robinson, "What the Lord Is Saying Today," His Kingdom Prophecy, September 7, 2015, https://www.hiskingdomprophecy.com/what-the-lord-is-saying-today-september-2015.

27

SABBATH: A CULTURE
The Jewish Story

> More than the Jews have kept the Sabbath, the Sabbath has kept the Jews.
>
> —Ahad Ha'am, pioneering Zionist and Hebrew writer

It was Friday, though not just any Friday. I was in Jerusalem, and I was about to be introduced to a cultural practice that has set God's people apart for three millennia. Sabbath was fast approaching. The shops had already closed, including "The Shuk," the famous fresh air market where hours before an elbow-room-only crowd of shoppers was purchasing foods of all kinds, spices galore, flowers ... oh, and don't forget the challah in preparation for the Shabbat dinner! Soon the hustle and bustle of preparation would be over. The streets would be empty of cars, buses, and taxis. What was left as the sun went down like a cloud of His presence hovering over this beautiful city was a holy hush. The busyness of life quickly paused—a "remember the Sabbath and keep it holy" stillness.

Even the hotels in Israel are equipped with Shabbat elevators. I inadvertently got on one before I realized they automatically stopped at every floor so the occupants don't have to "work" by pressing the buttons. This was such an intentional picture of "Slow down, Mary Jo. Take a deep breath. Receive this gift of time and rest." That evening at dinner I watched Jewish families gather around dining tables, generations old and young loving, laughing, lingering, and enjoying each other's company.

This outward, lived-out-loud faith was a very worshipful experience. It piqued my curiosity and then provoked me to jealousy. Yes, this Gentile was provoked to jealousy. I know Romans 11:11 speaks of the Jewish people being provoked to jealousy by the salvation and faith of the Gentiles, but in my case, it was the other way around. Not only did I love this public and private display of devotion to our God, but I also longed for it in my life and in the lives of others as well.

I had no way of knowing at that moment that I was only seeing the tip of the iceberg. The Jews' 24-hour Sabbath culture is the perfect tent of meeting (see Exodus 33:7–18). It represents leaving the busyness of life and pitching a camp to meet with God and have intentional communion time with Him. It includes enjoying His presence and listening to Him call me "friend." Oh yes, I was provoked to jealousy!

When I read Joe Lieberman's *The Gift of Rest,* it was awe-inspiring to take a close look inside the heart and mindset of his family. I began to see and understand the generational blessing that comes with observing the Sabbath so intentionally. My awakening was strengthened by reading Jewish cookbooks. I know this may surprise you, but I simply love them! The recipes include Sabbath stories from generations, so many different nations yet one people, that speak of the love, honor, blessing, and joy that come from God to these families. Sabbath truly kept them.

And here is one nugget, one piece of gold from this end of the rainbow covenant blessing: although Sabbath is only one day, the spirit of Sabbath is infused into every day of the week! Oh yes, Sabbath is one day, but the "remembering" and the "keeping" are all week long. We all know what it's like to have a wonderful time, a holiday meal, a birthday, or another special celebration with loved ones. It brings fellowship, love, laughter, and a shared experience that lingers long after the guests are gone and the family is tucked in bed. For the next several days we reflect on the memories made, the conversations had, and the blessed fellowship shared. Well, the same is true for Sabbath. Sunday, Monday, and Tuesday are marked as remembering days (see Exodus 20:8). Wednesday, Thursday, and Friday are the prepare-observe-keep mentioned in Deuteronomy 5:12. You see, "special" doesn't just happen; it takes planning, shopping, and preparing, and that's where the excitement and anticipation of the gathering time grows.

Making Sabbath a part of our lives takes intentionality. When I first began integrating the Sabbath into my life, I quickly discovered the busyness of the week didn't change. Friday night crept up on me, and I had nothing planned. Eventually I purchased a blackboard (intentional planning) sectioned off by lateral pieces of wood, one for each day of the week. Next to each day I wrote a word that would keep Sabbath on my mind:

- Sunday: Reset
- Monday: Remember
- Tuesday: Revelation
- Wednesday: Plan
- Thursday: Prep
- Friday: Presence (Bread)
- Saturday: Linger

Each week I fill in what do to that day—a Scripture to meditate on, a handwritten note to send, a meal to plan, guests to invite, etc.

The intentionality brings anticipation for the holy, set-apart day, which is then savored all week. It's so fun and yet so transformational. God used Sabbath to answer prayers I had prayed for years, many of which I didn't even know to pray!

About 20 years ago, after learning about Jewish tradition at their church, the Benjamin family decided to make the Sabbath a weekly part of their family life. This came as unwelcome news to the high school children who almost always had Friday night plans with sports and friends. The first dinner was met with resistance and long faces. But the atmosphere changed as candles were lit, communion was shared, and blessings were spoken from Gary (the father) over Jerri (the mother) and the children. At the second Sabbath, there was more family fun and conversation as the prayers and meal were enjoyed. On the third week, the parents told their children that they had a pre-commitment to a baby shower, so they would not be able to observe the Sabbath that Friday. By the children's reactions, you would have thought Gary and Jerri had cancelled the biggest holiday or birthday party ever! In fact, the youngest wanted a makeshift Sabbath dinner in the garage! Now, some 20-plus years later, the children are grown, and at last count, there are 16 grandchildren. Still, Sabbath is the weekly highlight of this generationally blessed family.

Gary told me of the miracles and countless answers to prayers that came as the generations sat around the Shabbat table to worship, pray, bless, and enjoy. There have been blessings of healings, births, and so much more! It reminded me of Genesis 18, when the three men met Abraham under the terebinth tree of Mamre. Abraham instructed Sarah to make bread while he prepared the dinner. Theologians speak of that meal, during which Jesus prophesied to Abraham that Sarah would have a child within the year, as being the first Sabbath dinner. And as the invited Guest at our Sabbaths today, Jesus is still speaking and blessing.

God is drawing both Jews and Gentiles to a fresh Sabbath awakening. In 2013 a chief rabbi from South Africa had the God-idea for The Shabbat Project. He called Jews of all backgrounds, beliefs, traditions, and ages to keep a full Sabbath together every year. The idea spread like wildfire to all corners of the world! Here in Dallas, Texas, people organized a challah bake, and 3,000 women gathered to learn how to make challah for their Shabbat dinner. A rabbi in San Francisco was interviewed about his reaction to the growing movement, and he said, "Anything that brings the Jewish people to the Sabbath table to talk of the coming Messiah is a good thing." To that I say amen! By the way, The Shabbat Project's website[18] welcomes viewers with a beautifully simple phrase: "Let the rhythm of Sabbath heal you." Another amen!

To address in just one chapter the culture of the Jewish people as they have embraced Sabbath over the millennia is daunting. What I hope I've been able to communicate to you is that this is truly a gift from God! We can learn so much from our Jewish brothers and sisters. Just look at the fruit of blessings that have kept these chosen ones together all these years. Yes, this grafted-in Gentile had a lot to learn. Let us not ignore that provoked-to-jealousy desire but instead hold it up as an offering and declare, "Teach us, Lord. Teach us!"

---

18. https://www.theshabbosproject.org/en/home

28

THE LION THAT ROARS

I saw a picture the other day of the head of a lion. Its glorious mane was transposed on a field of wheat ripe for harvest. It was such a dramatic picture of our Lion of Judah walking through the harvest-revival, prodigals-come-home, redeem-our-nation, heal-our-land fields. His very presence carried a sense of change in the air. There was such hope in the plowing, sowing, and watering, and now it's time to reap a move of God unlike anything the Church has known since Jesus Himself rose on Resurrection Sunday as our Lion of Judah!

Such a strong, prophetic picture caused the Spirit of God to rise within me. Oh, that we would get up off our knees and declare bold prayers that sound like the roar of our Lion of Judah. Our King of kings. Our Redeemer. Our Forerunner. We have the ultimate prayer partner in our Lord Jesus! It's imperative that we get our marching orders from the One who goes before us and declares this is His battle.

> The LORD says this to you: "Be not afraid or dismayed at this great multitude, for the battle is not yours, but God's" (2 Chronicles 20:15 AMP).

I'm reminded of something I learned in Israel that is so strategic about our position when praying for ... well, anything. We were in Israel at Tel Fahar where a memorial site had been erected to remember and honor the lives lost during the Six-Day War of 1967. Ilan Barkay, our tour guide, spoke with great solemnity and passion. After describing the character and courage of the Israeli military, he then mentioned the generals: "Our leaders, our generals, do not send their soldiers into battle. They go before them. They do not prepare strategy and then have others carry it out. They go first. The soldiers follow." This is our position, saints!

There are two wonderful, life-breathing, strategically anointed Scriptures that underscore how the banner we fight under is Jesus and we pray from the victory of the cross. In the first strategic Scripture, the prophet Micah speaks of Jesus' anointing where He goes before us and breaks up the way:

> The breaker [the Messiah, who opens the way] shall go up before them [liberating them].
> They will break out, pass through the gate and go out;
> So their King goes on before them,
> The Lord at their head (Micah 2:13 AMP).

I love the way my friend Rita prays. This single mother who is raising an adopted son has learned how to go boldly before the throne! Speaking of a difficult situation in which she was backed into a corner, my friend said to me, "I told the Lord He had 24 hours to fix this." Can you imagine? I love her boldness not birthed in an ounce of arrogance or disrespect. Rather, she was confident the Lord had directed her steps. He had opened all the right doors and even provided confirmation through a dream. This sudden situation was obviously a trap of the enemy; it had his fingerprints all over it. Every possible natural solution, opportunity, and idea had fallen through. But 23 hours and 15 minutes later, the problem was resolved in the most unlikely, miraculous, wouldn't-have-been-on-a list-of-100-options kind of way. Only God!

My friend didn't go into the final battle. Having already contended by faith, word, and actions what God had told her, she took off her prayer battle gear and put on praise. And Jesus, with His divine, breaker-finishing anointing, completed the good work He had begun.

The second strategic Scripture surprised me. I remember hearing someone pray about Jesus going before the Israelites as they passed though the Red Sea. I went to up to this person after the meeting and asked, "Where in the world did you find that in the Bible?" Sure enough, it is right there in Psalm 77:19:

> Your way [of escape for Your people] was through the sea,
> And Your paths through the great waters,
> And Your footprints were not traceable (AMP).

So often we cannot see what the Lord is doing, but all along He is there with us, going ahead of us and making a way.

All good soldiers need marching orders, and here is the way we receive ours:

1. *Ask*

> That night God appeared to Solomon. God said, "What do you want from me? Ask."
>
> God answered Solomon, "This is what has come out of your heart: You didn't grasp for money, wealth, fame, and the doom of your enemies; you didn't even ask for a long life. You asked for wisdom and knowledge so you could govern well my people

over whom I've made you king. Because of this, you get what you asked for—wisdom and knowledge. And I'm presenting you the rest as a bonus" (2 Chronicles 1:7, 11–12 MSG).

This may be sound oversimplified, but we do a lot of prayer-thinking and prayer-talking to others when the first and most important prayer should be a question: "Father, how do You want me to pray?" How does God see this situation? What do we need to know to pray effective, powerful, and righteous prayers? We don't ask often enough, and we don't ask soon enough. Many prayers never get asked at all! We hope. We ponder. We have faith. But until we speak, until we pray, things don't happen. Prayer is creative. Prayer is powerful. Prayer releases the will of God on earth. We may start our prayers from our soul (mind, will, and emotions), but when we engage with God, we shift from our soul to our spirit and begin to pray His will. You begin to pray what you see or hear God saying and doing, and that settles it. That's the power of praying through your spirit.

2. *Listen*

God will speak. Even in silence He is speaking. The Word of God is the light to our path (see Psalm 119:105). It is the source of wisdom and counsel, and it will tell you great and mighty things you don't know in the natural. I was praying through the family crisis I mentioned in "A Faith Trip to the Airport," and the trauma of the circumstances was paralyzing my prayers. I asked Father, "How do You want me to pray?" I got a picture of a courtroom where the judge and the lawyers went into the judge's chambers, so I prayed for the chamber-meeting. Fast forward a week later, I was sitting in the courtroom, and I watched the judge call counsel for both sides into chambers. I prayed in the Spirit and with understanding until they all returned to the courtroom. Then the judge issued a judgment that did not settle the case but most definitely was a breakthrough. (The case was settled and dismissed shortly after!)

3. Act

God will give us our marching orders. Sometimes the hardest order to obey is to wait. Wait on the Lord and renew your strength. He may tell you to fast. He may tell you to find an agreeing prayer partner. He may tell you to forgive. He may tell you to love more. You'll know. The Spirit of God will show you how to position yourself behind Jesus who has the breaker-anointing and goes before you! Our Savior-King always makes a way. He is "the way and the truth and the life" (John 14:6 NIV). He is our Lion of Judah, and His roar silences and scatters our enemy who prowls around, seeking someone to devour (see 1 Peter 5:8). We will not be shaken. We will not be moved. We are positioned behind the Lion of Judah! Amen!

29

BLESSED BY THE BREAD

Casey, my brother-in-the-Lord, made a bread board for me. (He also made my dining room table that I talk about in the "Sabbath: A Celebration" chapter.) On the bread board are these words in Hebrew: "Send Forth the Bread." We carry the Bread of Life, the presence of God, in us wherever we go. Digging a little into the Hebrew meaning of "send," I found "begin," and that's where this book started—"Begin with Bread!" "Send forth" reminds me of "cast your bread upon the waters" in Ecclesiastes 11:1. We cast our cares on God knowing He will take care of us. We cast our nets where God tells us to pray, love, and serve. We cast our bread by sharing His presence (and in my case, literal bread) to bless the receiver. What a picture of us sharing what God has put in our hands and sending it forth for Him to bless others!

Challah is so much more than a recipe—it's a love offering to the Lord. It's all about the Bread of Life (Jesus) and making a place for the presence of God in our every day. The anointing on this simple but profound act of baking bread has an ingredient that cannot be listed in a recipe. It can only be the Spirit of God capturing the hearts of men and women.

Early on I began doing what I call "porch drops." I made challah for people who were sick, graduating, celebrating a birthday ... any occasion was enough reason. I would wrap it up and put it in a white bag with a label that says, "Begin with bread" and a little bit of tissue paper. Then I left it on front porches with a note. Being able to share the joy of challah bread has been such a bonus, and the testimonies of this movement that God started have a life of their own! God is inspiring people in the ways they can cast their bread upon the water, send forth the bread, and carry His presence. It's a beautiful thing to watch unfold, and we are just at the beginning! I hope some of these testimonies will inspire you.

A friend shared a story about her sister, her husband, and their three elementary school-aged children. The husband was having major kidney issues and needed a transplant. It was very hard on him and his family. My friend took food over to help them and included challah bread. Finally, her sister asked, "Do you pray over the bread when you make it? Because every time you make the bread my house is so peaceful, the kids don't fight, and things always seem to be so much better." My friend replied, "Yes, I pray over you and your family as I am making the bread." All her sister could say was "Thank you" and "Can you make the bread more often?"

This story reminded me just how amazing our heavenly Father is. When we speak with Him, He always listens. He goes before us and touches lives all because we asked. He is so good! My friend shared, "Learning to make bread and pray while I'm baking ... and taking the presence of God into my sister's home ... Well, it's affecting all the lives around me!"

Luciana, a young lady from Costa Rica, attended an Acts 2:42 Challah-Day. Returning home, she and her sister decided to start making bread for sale but with a purpose. Every person who purchased challah would receive a digital note explaining how they were prayed for during the baking process.

> While we add every ingredient to our challah, we pray that God blesses you. That the word of the living WATER nourishes you and blesses you abundantly, so it flows to others as well. That your family, friendships, and those who you share this bread with grow (yeast) spiritually in all their potential and that new blessings hatch (eggs) in your life so that God reveals everything that is to come. That the anointment (oil) of the Lord covers you and your faith (sugar) grows so that you face any situation with joy knowing that they're for good. That your life is purified (salt) so nothing toxic arrives in your life, mind, soul, and body. And that the nourishment (flour) will be used for good.

Years later Luciana got married. Not only did she make challah bread for her communion ceremony, but she also made enough to be distributed among her 100 guests so they could share in this covenant act. The presence of God filled the room!

One more story, though I could listen to these testimonies all day long! Recently, a local synagogue was under siege. A gunman held four men (before releasing one) for hours. It captured the attention of the world. Gratefully, the rabbi and two remaining men were able to escape before the situation escalated. It was 11 hours of trauma for the men held captive, their families, the synagogue members, and the Beth Israel community!

Anne, a friend who had attended one of my Challah-Days, responded by making challah bread for one of her Jewish neighbors who is part of the Beth Israel community. As she was praying and kneading, a deep love and care for this congregation gripped her. She delivered the bread with a loving note:

> Numbers 6:24–26: "The Lord bless you and keep you; the Lord make his face shine on you and be gracious to you; the Lord turn his face toward you and give you peace."

The recipient neighbor was so surprised and honored by this kind gesture, and she even asked for the recipe!

Friends, challah breads have made their way to weddings, showers, and endless special occasions. Children are even asking their mothers to help them make some for sick friends! And people are asking, "Can you teach me?"

I would never want to limit this just to baking bread. Remember, more than a loaf of bread, we are carriers of the presence of God. We are watching God, in new and unusual ways, move people to share His presence. I'm thinking of praying groups that go to hospitals and sit in the parking lots or walk around the building. They pray that those inside would be touched by God, Jesus would reveal Himself to them, and they would be healed and made whole.

We are being charged to be the Church outside the walls. Just as the Church responded to the COVID shutdown through phone calls and prayers that deeply touched people's lives and brought them God's peace, we are being challenged in new ways to go into our schools, neighborhoods, and communities. God is giving us an opportunity to bloom in places we didn't even know He was planting us! I pray that these testimonies of people being blessed by the physical kindness of bread shared will inspire you. There is no limit to the way God wants to use you and your gifts in others' lives. You are a blessing!

30

KICKING AGAINST THE GOADS

A *piano recital.* The very thought fills me with dread now almost as much as it did when I was in third grade in Catholic school. Week after week, little Mary Jo climbed the three daunting flights of stairs reserved for upperclassmen. I entered the long, narrow room and walked to the platform where the piano sat. Next to the piano was my teacher, Mrs. Smith, with the proverbial ruler in her hand.

It was my last practice before the big day: my first public performance at the keys. I fumbled through my assigned musical piece, making one mistake after another. The more I messed up, the more intimidated and fearful I became. I timidly suggested to Mrs. Smith an alternative piece, which I proceeded to play perfectly. My earnest appeal to change the selected piece to one I was more comfortable with fell on deaf ears.

On the day of the presentation, I walked through the long, narrow room flanked by rows of nuns and parents. My turn came, and Mrs. Smith introduced me and the originally planned piece. I confidently proceeded to sit down and *play the piece I wanted to play. The perfect piece.* Only this time it was not perfect. I messed it up in a grand way, and my confidence gave way to tears that splashed onto the keys. Mrs. Smith, gracious in words but with a stern voice, stopped me mid-score. She then reintroduced me and the *assigned piece*. And I played it perfectly.

Why did this feels-like-it-just-happened-yesterday illustration come to mind as I wrestled with God? He was directing me to do something, but I felt unqualified. I was certain everyone—anyone—could do better. I measured my value not as God measures but rather as one would measure a cup of flour for a recipe. I did my best to ignore, resist, and argue against the assignment.

Then the phrase "kicking against the goads" came to mind. I knew it was from somewhere in Scripture, and sure enough I found it in Acts 26:14: "It is hard for you to kick against the goads" (ESV). The next thing the Lord whispered was, "Mary, get ready to repent." Oh, He sounded just like Mrs. Smith!

But what is a goad? A goad is a pointed stick used for prodding, guiding, and steering oxen in the desired direction when plowing the fields. Dare I say that oxen are known to be stubborn? Ouch! And when a stubborn ox resists and kicks back, it only inflicts more pain upon itself.

This is exactly what can happen when we rebel, resist, or are just plain stubborn against what God is asking or directing us to do. Our resistance may be based in insecurity, fear of man, or intimidation. Have you been there? Done that? The assignment could be to join the altar ministry, call someone to pray for them, or become part of a prayer meeting and, heaven-forbid, pray out loud! It could be going to that nation, teaching that class, leading that group, taking that job, forgiving that person. I hesitate to list the "here I have sent them" scenarios, but I know you get the idea!

These are the times when God is saying, "I know the plans for well-being, a future, and a hope. Call to me, and I will answer and tell you great and mighty things" (see Jeremiah 29:11; 33:3). However, what He proposes doesn't always sound much like well-being or great things. It's so much easier to shrink back into the comfortable, safe boundaries in which we thrive.

But the truth is this: living prayer means going where we are not comfortable, praying for people for whom we don't feel qualified to pray, and taking God-appointed and anointed assignments that are beyond our natural ability. God did not ask us to live prayer in our comfort zone. In fact, it's outside our comfort zone where the Holy Spirit moves and breathes and makes God's presence and power manifest.

Please don't limit this to something God asks, directs, or requires of you publicly. It may very well be something private— between you and God. We serve and pray to a big God. (What an understatement!) We also have a comfort zone in our prayer life with God, which usually involves *not* asking with bold, strong prayers. I remember Lisa Bevere speaking about a time she and her husband, John, were praying for a ministry goal. They decided to pray for double or triple or something out of the possible. She said, "We prayed a prayer that scared what was scared inside of us.... If it doesn't scare you, it's not scaring the enemy."[19] Our yielding to what is uncomfortable for us or praying what is impossible to us puts us in the position to agree with God. The Word instructs us to be bold, persistent, brave, and strong in asking for God to move.

Oh, one other thing about the beloved, stubborn oxen: there are two yoked together. And that is where we place ourselves

---

19. James Robison, "Lisa Bevere: Scary Prayers," LIFE Today, YouTube video, 2:14, July 11, 2012, https://www.youtube.com/watch?v=vDaFH3aN4wY.

when we yield to the impossible. God is directing our steps and our prayers to be yoked to His plans, purposes, and timing. When we resist Him, are we not *unequally yoked?* You hear that term often in romantic relationships between believers and unbelievers, but such is the case here too. When we yield to trusting God, it becomes the best "where two or more agree" situation there is.

Our living prayer is the very essence of our relationship and partnership with God—Father, Jesus, and Holy Spirit. Trusting God is the key to praying His will, His Word, His wisdom, and His power into our prayer assignments. When you feel resistance in your mind, will, or emotions, then it's time to stop and ask God why you are so resistant to His voice. Then determine to trust Him and obey.

> Your ears shall hear a word behind you, saying
> "This *is* the way, walk in it" (Isaiah 30:21).

> Eye has not seen, nor ear heard,
> Nor have entered into the heart of man
> The things which God has prepared for those who love Him
> (1 Corinthians 2:9).

> If any of you lacks wisdom, let him ask of God, who gives to all liberally and without reproach, and it will be given to him (James 1:5).

Lord, I'll admit it is often easy to be like Gideon and look over my shoulder, certain You are speaking to someone else. And yet, there is a growing sense of anticipation and excitement when I find myself courageous enough to link arms with You and obey that still, small voice that often becomes a thunder. I trust You and Your Word, and I desire my life of living prayer to be a reflection of Joshua, who was brave and strong and took the land.

Then He will give the rain
for your seed
With which you sow the ground,
And bread of the increase
of the earth;
It will be fat and plentiful.
In that day your cattle will feed
In large pastures.

Isaiah 30:23

31

TRUST THE WIND

A 30"x30" picture of a boat hangs in my study. It reads, "Trust that the wind knows where it's going." The MJP translation is "Trust the leading of the Holy Spirit." Trust the timing of the Holy Spirit. Trust that He is keeping us in the center of God's perfect will. Trust that we recognize His voice.

Meteorologists test the wind by using instruments and even resort to the tried-and-true wet index finger in the air to feel the direction of the wind. We have a "tester" too! He's the Holy Spirit.

Recently, I found myself in a two-and-a-half-year conversation regarding the timing and perfect will of God. My journals have multiple entries mentioning just this. Walk through my Hugging Bible, and you will see Scriptures highlighted and marked with dates that kept this conversation going. I knew the timing mattered. It mattered to God. It mattered to me. It involved a major life transition where being in the perfect timing of God was paramount. Not too early. Not too late.

As I was anchored in my prayer chair, God knew circumstances were about to unfold that would require a decision from me. I specifically asked God how He wanted to begin our conversation that day. I immediately sensed the wind-whisper, followed by the word "crossroads." That was out of nowhere. Crossroads had not been part of any conversation to date! So what did I do? I chose to ignore it. Instead, I selected a favorite conversation starter: *appointed time*. In fancy, bold calligraphy letters, I scripted *Appointed Time*. Then I waited. And waited. And waited. Silence.

Interrupted by my phone, I glanced down and saw a text message that said:

CROSSROADS. CROSSROADS. Make a choice. Don't go backwards. There are new places, new revelation, new ways of praying ... CROSSROADS.

"Crossroads" was bolded, underlined, and italicized! God wanted to continue our conversation that day with crossroads. Well, okay then! I did a Scripture search to see if I could find a reference.

Stand at the crossroads and look;
   ask for the ancient paths,
ask where the good way is, and walk in it,
   and you will find rest for your souls (Jeremiah 6:16 NIV).

The Holy Spirit's wind-whisper just became a shout: *This is the way, now walk in it!* That was it. Decision made. Choice made. Settled in heaven and on earth. That two-and-a-half-year pondering now had a definitive answer.

Compare this to a time my husband and I were considering a purchase (a want, not a need). We allowed our want to drown out any chance of hearing the Holy Spirit. We decided if such and such fell into place, then that was God's "yes." Well, such and such did fall into place, and it took us nearly three years to undo our want. Three years to live out the consequences of not giving room for the Holy Spirit's discernment. Not asking what God wanted us to do.

In this rapidly ever-changing world, learning to discern the will of our Father is imperative. Since the beginning of time, it's been important for God's people to hear His voice and obey. Just ask Abraham where he would live. Or Joseph where he should work. Or Mary on whom she would marry and when she would start a family. How about you? Is the Holy Spirit your GPS of choice? How does He counsel and direct you? How have you learned to discern the difference between God's voice, your voice, and the enemy's voice?

The best way to learn the voice of the Holy Spirit is pinpoint obedience. When the Holy Spirit whispers or nudges or brings a directive to mind, respond with quick obedience. Over time you will learn to discern between a good idea versus a God-directive. God wants to establish you in each season of your life and in all your decisions, big and small.

Develop a prayer practice to discern and distinguish the voice of the Spirit. This takes time. His voice competes with the voices of others in this world, including the enemy. At times it will take a *rhema* (God's directive though His written Word) Scripture to settle things. Sometimes God arranges circumstances beyond our control, but they are accompanied with confidence that He went before us. And in times like this He will use an unaware friend to send a divinely orchestrated text message. God's methods are not all the same, but His voice, prompting, nudge, or sign is your compass.

Finding your "this is the way, now walk in it" directive is not necessarily a short conversation. In fact, it probably will be the opposite when you are seeking God's will and purpose for a spouse, a school, a job, a home, a ministry, a child, a relationship ... the list goes on and on. Life continually presents us with eternal decisions—ones that will chart our course, make a world of difference, and impact not just us but those around us too.

> But the Helper, the Holy Spirit, whom the Father will send in my name, he will teach you all things and bring to your remembrance all that I have said to you (John 14:26 ESV).

> My sheep hear My voice, and I know them, and they follow Me (John 10:27).

Father, I trust You for the timing of answers and even the way You choose to answer! That's part of the adventure in praying. The waiting is hard. The contrary voices are distracting. The confusion is discouraging. But more than anything I desire and need Your perfect will for my life. So I will ask, believe, wait. and obey. Thank You, Jesus, for mediating on my behalf. Thank You, Holy Spirit, for teaching me how You speak and confirming this is the way, now walk in it. In Jesus' name, Amen.

32

JUST SAY YES

> For all the promises of God find their Yes in him. That is why it is through him that we utter our Amen to God for his glory.
>
> —2 Corinthians 1:20 (ESV)

This prayer, obedience, and following the voice of God story is about two men: my 86-year-old husband, Bruce, and his 26-year-old friend, John Austin. The setting is a wedding. Not just any wedding, though; this one is extra special. Bruce is officiating his first "I now pronounce you husband and wife" ceremony. Covenant vows are about to be exchanged in front of an arch of fresh spring flowers set under the massive branches of a generations-old, 70-foot-tall, 120-inch-wide oak tree.

What brought these three people together on this most sacred occasion? It's more fitting to ask, "Who?" God's hand was certainly at work. It all started when Bruce, a professor of American history, and John Austin, a freshman Bible college student, met. What began as a classroom friendship evolved when John Austin asked Bruce, "Would you pray about mentoring me?" John Austin had sat in Bruce's classes and seen a man who integrated his relationship with Jesus into every facet of his life, class, and the material being taught. John Austin heard and saw a man who valued character far above achievement. And from the other direction, Bruce saw a young man leaning into God. He saw someone with a listening ear and an open heart—a future husband and father who desired above all to learn to walk and lead in the ways of God.

God's answer to both men's prayers was a definitive *yes*. A gap of 60 years was bridged by a common love of God, the pursuit of a personal relationship with Jesus, and the willingness to obey the Holy Spirit's promptings. Over the next five years, countless lunchtime conversations were spent discussing a close, surrendered walk with Jesus and praying together. They prayed for wisdom and counsel. They prayed for direction for so many life decisions, including John Austin's desire for a perfect, God-the-best-Matchmaker-sent wife.

Bruce's "yes" to the request for mentoring followed a series of yeses, each a result of prayer and a willingness to live outside his personal comfort zone:

- Yes, when God asked him, a recently retired 39-year military and commercial pilot, to return to college and finish his bachelor's degree.
- Yes, when God directed him to pursue a masters in Christian ministry and history, only to graduate 14 months later at the ripe young age of 74.
- Yes, to an offer to become an adjunct professor just three weeks after graduation.

Similarly, John Austin had a series of yeses:

- Yes, to trusting God for provision at the Bible college and no to full-ride scholarships elsewhere.
- Yes, to asking an older, wiser man to mentor and challenge him in areas of his life in need of iron sharpening iron.

- Yes, to a God-directed move away from family, friends, church, and a planned career for a new job in a new city.

Of course, God had the final "yes." This new job in this new city afforded John Austin the opportunity to pursue the heart of Kenna Marie. This young woman is so special, so set apart for God, and so in love with Jesus and the Word. As Bruce said during the ceremony, "It's hard to improve on perfection." The two are truly God's perfect match.

So there stands a proud officiant watching the radiant bride listen intently as her beaming groom speaks the most powerful oath he will ever make. The exchange is complete when she returns her words of covenant promise. Kenna's tears mixed with deep joy wrap the listeners in a literal holy hush.

My own tears mix with deep joy as I pray for these precious three who said yes to God. Under the umbrella of the breathtaking old tree, I am reminded of the oaks of righteousness written about in Isaiah 61:3:

> They will be called oaks of righteousness,
> A planting of the Lord
> for the display of his splendor (NIV).

Indeed, these three were brought together by the Lord for His glory.

Your yeses to God don't have to make sense. Time. Age. Distance. Comfort zone. Life experiences. Current demands. Personal limitations. These may all be reasons that you may well *reason* a no. Prayerfully seeking God's heart will ultimately lead you to discover His perfect plans and purposes. We don't have to understand the whole of our yeses. We just need to know He's the one asking!

Don't shrink back! God has invested in you, and He will offer you opportunities to share your "talent" (Matthew 25:14–30) with others. Take a few moments this day or this week to read and ponder the following verses. Let them get into your spirit and soul so that when He asks, you will be ready with an exuberant "Yes!"

> Whether *it is* pleasant or unpleasant, we will listen to the voice of the Lord our God to whom we are sending you, so that it may go well with us when we listen to the voice of the Lord our God (Jeremiah 42:6 NASB).

> Give instruction to a wise man and he will be still wiser, Teach a righteous man and he will increase his learning (Proverbs 9:9 ESV).

> And even when *I am* old and gray, God, do not abandon me, Until I declare Your strength to *this* generation, Your power to all who are to come (Psalm 71:18 NASB).

> As for the things you have learned and received and heard and seen in me, practice these things, and the God of peace will be with you (Philippians 4:9 NASB).

> But the noble person devises noble plans; And by noble plans he stands (Isaiah 32:8 NASB).

Lord, it's one thing to pray, but it's an entirely other thing to be willing to be the answer to someone's prayer. I want to be that person who prays, whether praying for You to strengthen my walk or praying to strengthen the walks of others. In saying yes, I trust that You will provide the wisdom, the strength, the time, the heart, the compassion … the whatever is needed! I desire to walk in prayerful obedience and glorify You in the process! I love You, Lord! In Jesus' name, Amen.

33

TOO GOOD NOT TO GIVE IT AWAY

> They were continually devoting themselves to the apostles' teaching and to fellowship, to the breaking of bread and to prayer.
>
> —Acts 2:42 (NASB)

I've always been of the mindset that what God gives to us, we give away to others. While I am not an authority on any given subject, I may know a little more than someone else. Like baking bread! My introduction to how our Jewish brothers and sisters observe and celebrate Sabbath both intrigued and inspired me, and it ignited a desire to learn and glean from them. I knew they had something I wanted and needed—a pace and rhythm to their life, a devotion to God that lived their faith out loud, and a biblical value that honored Him. And bread baking? What a bonus!

As soon as I learned about Sabbath and baking challah, I knew I wanted to share it with others. However, I definitely didn't think I would come to welcome close to 700 men, women, and children into my home to learn about the Shabbat dinner and challah. And that's just the number at the time of writing this book. There are hundreds more who have contacted me and said they would like to come. It speaks to the growing desire God has put in us for intentional Sabbath and the bread of His presence.

I want to encourage you to become a student *and* a teacher, a disciple of these truths God is writing on the hearts of believers around the world. What I am about to share is the format I use for my Acts 2:42 Challah-Days. You can adapt this to a couple, a home group, a shower, a party—any setting, really! There is no limit to the ways you can share this. It can be done at a marriage retreat or having couples over for a mini retreat. I have had families, women's groups, church departments, engagement and wedding showers, girls whose mothers wanted me to mentor them ... the joy-list goes on!

Let's take a peek into one of my "Challah-Days":

Click. Click. Click. I am sitting in my living room listening to the rhythmic sound of my metronome as a group greets one another, grabs hot cups of coffee, and acclimates to the surroundings of my home. *Click. Click. Click.* It takes a few minutes, but each person eventually turns their attention to the sound of the metronome. It draws them in. *Click. Click. Click.* They begin taking their places with their beverages, Bibles, and journals. A hush falls over the room, and the metronome plays on for several minutes, issuing an invitation. We begin to sense the presence of God drawing us in. They say one picture is worth 1,000 words, but today, it is one small instrument that speaks loud and clear—a visual and audio lesson of Sabbath rest.

The metronome, which normally sits on the windowsill in my prayer room, has always represented to me the heartbeat of God. It syncs my heartbeat to His, whether living in a time of extreme busyness and needing grace-to-grace for the race or slowing down to the heartbeat of Sabbath. One this day, my

20 special guests and I are going to live Acts 2:42—teaching, fellowship, breaking (and making) of bread, and prayer.

We have a schedule for the day, but the boss of the clock is the bread because it requires time to rest and rise (proof). The same application goes for hosting the presence of God. We have a schedule, but our primary focus is to yield to the leading of the Holy Spirit. Sabbath-pondering requires time to rest, pause, lean in, and listen. It requires time for the principles to take up residence in our hearts as we rise to making the Sabbath a delight.

Challah-Day is all hands-on deck. There are absolutely no spectators! We're not there to merely learn about Sabbath, making bread, and prayer, but also to have fun doing it. We are gathered to receive an impartation, a new or deeper revelation of living prayer. We will do that through the rest of God found in the spirit of Sabbath (not just the day). We will dig a little deeper into the generational blessing the Jewish people have in preparing challah and discover for ourselves the joy of prayer-baking! There will be time to pause and journal and ask God key questions about what we are experiencing.

Now off to the kitchen we go. Each person goes to my Shabbat pantry to select an apron. You may ask, "What is a Shabbat pantry?" Simply put, it is everything I will need to set a table and bake bread in one place! Tablecloths on pull-out rods, napkins, bread-rising towels, pitchers for Shabbat flowers, flour, sugar, yummy fillings for the bread, and way too many aprons! (Can a girl really have too many aprons, though?)

Picture, if you will, 20 people standing around my kitchen island, and all of them, even the guys, donning ruffled, flowery aprons. Let the fun begin! For the next 30–45 minutes, I stand to the side and act as a conductor as each participant engages in mixing the wet and dry ingredients. And yes, we do have a one-handed egg cracking contest! Over the course of the day (broken up by lunch, journaling, and fellowship), each person mixes, kneads, and braids. If you could only hear the ooohhhhs and ahhhhs as the bread comes out of the oven. There is such joy in seeing their completed special creation!

I write about the actual challah-making experience in another chapter. But please hear me: the 100 percent consensus of the group speaks of encountering the presence of God, the delight of God, and the joy of connecting with God in a very Brother Lawrence way (while doing a chore or a mundane task). This is living prayer in an intimate way!

The bread recipe calls for two times of rest: the first approximately two hours and the second approximately one hour. During the rest times, we have lunch or snacks (depending on the time of day). The real bonus is having time to process and journal what God is saying. Each person leaves with a plan—a Sabbath plan for their lives!

Psalm 17:15 speaks of seeing God face to face and having sweet communion with Him. Today we encounter our own burning bush, face-to-face time with God. Don't be surprised at what can happen in a crowded place as well as in the quiet of your prayer chair! Throughout the day, we laugh, pray, knead, bake, journal, and inquire of the Lord what the fourth commandment (keeping the Sabbath holy) looks like in our lives. We graft ourselves into the blessing of challah baking and weekly Sabbath meal traditions. In a grand finale, we gather around the table to light candles, worship, pray, take communion, bless one another, and enjoy. What a day!

If you want to do this yourself, I recommend starting with a very flexible itinerary. Here is the one I use for the people who come into my home for a Challah-Day:

- Welcome and Introduction to Sabbath—15 minutes
  You'll find great teaching points in my chapters on Sabbath.
- Making Challah—45 minutes (depending on group size)
  You'll find great teaching points in my chapters on challah.
- First Rise—2 hours
- Lunch, fellowship, and teaching (question and answer time included)
- Second Rise—1 hour (include 15 minutes for braiding)
- Individual processing, journaling, and pondering
- Baking—30 minutes
  I use this time to go over the Sabbath meal (covered in the "Sabbath: A Celebration" chapter) and prayer. There is also time to pray for the attendees or pray for each other.
- Celebration at Shabbat Table—as long as you would like!

This day is about teaching, fellowship, baking bread, and prayer. But even more than what we do, it is all about whom we host—the Holy Spirit. Twenty or so years ago I read a book by Ché Ahn, titled *Hosting the Holy Spirit*. I went to revisit the book and found this note written by me on the inside cover:

> Awoke from a dream saying to someone, "I am an agent of the Holy Spirit. Through hospitality I am going to clean the plaque out of your heart, and you too will be able to host the Holy Spirit."

I have seen this demonstrated over and over again as the Holy Spirit ministers to men, women, and children. Making challah is not a "girl thing"; it's not even about making bread. It's about cultivating the presence of God. I wish I could share all the testimonies I have received from both men and women about how their lives have been changed by the Sabbath. What a blessing to get text messages and photos of families making challah and gathering for Shabbat. Parents are teaching their children, and people are inviting their neighbors and prayer groups into their homes. Friend, it doesn't get any better than that! I encourage and challenge you to open your heart and your home to the Sabbath. As my friend Tiffany told me, "The day may start out as mundanely as asking my husband to get a stick of butter out, but when we make challah, something special happens *every time*." This is the perfect picture of a life of prayer. Let it rise!

34

OUR LIFE, A GRAIN OFFERING

Recently, the enemy, the accuser, came in like a flood. I recognized his voice. Dream stealer. Purpose killer. Faith and hope destroyer. Every sin, memories long forgotten, surfaced.

My mind was the battlefield. And yet I knew my spiritual address was not defeat, discouragement, or depression. So I prayed in the Spirit and with understanding. I took communion. I hugged my Bible and meditated on Scriptures to bring faith, hope, love, forgiveness, mercy, and grace.

> And the Lord said, "Simon, Simon! Indeed, Satan has asked for you, that he may sift *you* as wheat. But I have prayed for you, that your faith should not fail; and when you have returned to *Me,* strengthen your brethren" (Luke 22:31–32).

Sifting? The enemy's plan when sifting us is to try to make us focus on temporary, earthly things. God has a better plan, though. Another word for sifting is threshing, and some wonderful things happen when we submit to God's plan for "threshing"—the good remains, and our lives become a sacrificial grain offering.

Biblically speaking, a grain offering is a sacrifice. It is a picture of our Lord on the cross. His was the ultimate sacrifice—the very Bread of Life offered up for you and me. Hebrews 13:15 instructs us, "By Him [Jesus] let us continually offer the sacrifice of praise to God." Even when the enemy comes in like a flood, we are strengthened by the Lord in faith. Whether we approach the throne room with broken and fragmented hearts or with boldness and confidence, our God awaits us as we offer a sacrifice of thanksgiving and praise.

Ezekiel 46:14 speaks of the fine flour in the grain offering, which comes from refining and threshing. Let's look at the place where threshing happens—the holy, pressed-down, shaken-together, and poured-out place with God.

Practically, the threshing floor represents a place of **separation**. It is on the threshing floor that farmers took the sheaves of wheat and, through a crushing process, separated the grain (good part) from the husk (the chaff). Then, with a winnowing fork, the grain would be tossed into the air, the chaff would float away, and what remained was the valuable part.

Spiritually, the threshing floor is a place of intercession (mediation), humility, and revelation. Where we meet with God, humble ourselves, work out His will, and hear His voice. Where our place of sacrifice becomes our place of worship!

You'll love this! The Temple was built on a threshing floor. It began when Abraham took Isaac to Mount Moriah for the ultimate sacrifice of his promised covenant son. The Lord redeemed the sacrifice of obedience with a ram. Later, King David purchased the threshing floor of Araunah the Jebusite on Mount Moriah to stop the Angel of Death who was exacting punishment for sin (2 Samuel 24:18–25). And it was on this site that Solomon eventually began building the Temple to honor

God (see 2 Chronicles 3:1). *Abraham's original threshing floor of sacrifice ultimately became the place of worship!*

Sometimes the threshing floor can be our kitchen. A friend relays the following story:

> I had a dream last night. I was in this dreamy kitchen: so big, so clean, and beautiful. Then I saw you and me in that kitchen. We were kneading dough, challah dough. I remember you telling me, "Whenever you are having a troubled situation, make challah, because making challah is like making warfare, or even intercession."
>
> At the beginning of this week, I had a time of adversity, which brought me to my knees in prayer. Immediately after I went into my kitchen, and I felt this need to make challah. Instead, I began with the daily chores like cleaning and laundry. God used you to remind me about the beautiful benefit (as the Bible says) of meeting the Lord in the challah-making process. This couple of months have been so rough for our family, and personally I have been struggling with this battlefield that is the mind. But thanks to your message, I remembered, and yesterday I made challah. Oh friend, I just felt the presence of the Holy Spirit, and all those thoughts were gone!

Working with the finest flour at her threshing floor (kitchen), my friend's life became a grain offering, and she had two beautiful loaves of challah too!

This next testimony from my friend Tiffany Buchanan will encourage and inspire us. Once again, God uses the actual making of the bread to meet with us at the threshing floor.

> Last night I told Phil that I just felt so defeated, and I was trying to figure out why. Probably a combination of a lot of

"life" factors and having a very full plate at work. I just felt defeated. I still felt that way this morning. With Phil at work and the three children at school, I had about 30 minutes before my first meeting. I felt the Lord say, "Make challah." It's been 1–2 months since I have made it because life has busy, and I have been tired.

So I got to it! As I was rolling and braiding, my eyes were FILLED with tears, and my heart was FILLED with so many thoughts about the goodness of God in mine and my family's life ... even when I feel tired and defeated. My literal tears are in the bread today, and it speaks more to my heart than I can even put to words. And not just that. My brain had so much going on in there, and I felt so much peace. Things that felt fuzzy felt clear!

While the bread itself is so good, it's way more than just making bread. It's how the Lord speaks to me in ways that I need!

When we are being sifted and crushed on the threshing floor, we turn to God for the separating of wheat from chaff. We offer our praises of thanksgiving. We encourage ourselves by remembering that the Lord is taking our lives and turning them into a fine grain offering. Our grain offering, like bread, is what we sacrificially offer to our Lord, trusting He will work *all* things for the good. Because we do love Him. And we are called to His purposes (see Romans 8:28).

35

SABBATH: A CELEBRATION
Our Story

I have a very fond memory of one Sabbath evening when I was in Israel on a prayer-worship pilgrimage. We were about to have dinner, and behind our team were two elongated tables filled to overflowing with a family's laughter and lively conversation. Then a holy hush came over the group. The matriarch lit candles and prayed. The patriarch stood and prayed a short prayer. What happened next pierced my heart and solidified my quest to embrace the whole of what God was teaching me about Shabbat.

The family members began to bless one another. We watched as mothers and fathers gently cupped the faces of their children, and spouses lovingly embraced and whispered to one another. Uncles, aunts, grandparents, and cousins all participated in this wonderful moment in which God paused time for the sharing of honor and affirmation. It was as beautiful as any sunset or sunrise I ever saw, and it was as moving as any wedding ceremony. Following this holy blessing everyone took their seats. For the remainder of the evening meal, they shared laughter, stories, and spirited conversations.

I was deeply moved. I had an instant awareness of the power of this sacred moment, and I knew I wanted what they had. I returned home with a renewed personal commitment to figure it out. One thing I knew for sure was that this life-changing lesson would be taught by the Spirit, because it was a work of the Spirit. But where do you start?

I decided to begin with something tangible: a dining table. I spent months looking through Pinterest, and one day I found exactly what I was looking for: a table made with huge planks of barn wood and a gorgeous crystal chandelier hanging over it. I thought, *That's it!* The handcrafted table represented humility, and the chandelier—the biggest I could afford and the largest my ceiling could accommodate—represented the glory of God hanging over my family and guests.

I texted my friend Casey, "Will you make me a Shabbat table?" He probably wondered, *What is she thinking*? as he replied, "Let's talk." After we talked about my desires for this dining table, Casey found the materials: oak for the tabletop, cedar for the table's apron, and sycamore for the table's legs. Each wood had a biblical basis. I also wanted to incorporate the words worship, pray, bless, and enjoy. I selected these four after observing, participating, and reading about Shabbat. They are my adaptation of the Jewish Sabbath practices and prayers. Casey fire-branded the four words in Hebrew on the corners of the table. He then branded each of the sycamore legs with a single Hebrew letter that spelled out *Yod-Hei-Vav-Hei*, which translates to "LORD, eternal God, the I AM." The table and chandelier represent our Lord Jesus and how God sent Him from heaven to earth—from glory to humility and back to glory again.

Shortly after, we had a workman lay wood floors in our dining room. I thanked him for taking such care and wrapping the chandelier. Although we spoke different languages, I took him to the table and explained with my best hand motions, "Dinner. Daddy. Momma. Children. Pray." This man's response brought me to tears. He threw himself with outstretched arms onto my table and hugged it. Friends, this is one of countless examples of the anointing the Sabbath carries. It's not just a table. It's an altar of worship.

Do you need Casey to build you a table in order to have Sabbath in your home? Of course not. Your table is as anointed as mine. This special place to gather and invite the very presence of Jesus, our special Guest, to the meal is a holy, devoted place. I have countless testimonies of God's anointing on the Sabbath—from making the challah, to the preparations, to the gathering, to the prayers, to the laughter and love, etc. It literally defies description.

My dear friend Bonnie Saul Wilks authored *Sabbath: A Gift of Time*.[20] This is a must-read primer. Not only does she lay a biblical foundation for Sabbath, but she offers the reader a step-by-step guide for the Shabbat meal (recipes included) and prayers.

You may be wondering what a typical Shabbat gathering looks like at my house. It is based on the four words I previously mentioned: worship, pray, bless, and enjoy. These four words are the corners of my table and the corners of Sabbath celebration. After the guests have arrived and the food has been placed on the table next to the candles, it is time to begin. The atmosphere is charged with expectation. After all, this is no ordinary dinner. Join me at my table, will you?

---

20. Bonnie Saul Wilks, *Sabbath: A Gift of Time* (Southlake, TX: Gateway Publishing, 2018).

Worship

I open Shabbat dinner with my favorite Sabbath worship leader, Marty Goetz, playing the "Hebrew Chant" followed by "Show Me Thy Glory." You can feel the inaudible sighs around the table as we let go of the week and enter into His rest. Selah! A few minutes into the second song, I turn the volume down and light the candles.

Following the tradition of Jewish matriarchs, I welcome our guests, and more importantly, the Guest of Honor, Jesus, with three circular waves of my arms. Then I close my eyes and say a prayer. It is not a memorized prayer but rather a prayer from my heart welcoming the Lord of the Sabbath—Jesus, our Light of the world. I may mention He is the Light penetrating darkness, the Word who lights our path, and the Sabbath Rest we are seeking.

Pray

My husband then takes the two loaves of challah (two because of the double manna God provided in the wilderness for 40 years so the Jewish people would not work on Sabbath). What a beautiful picture and reminder of God's provision! Bruce prays a prayer from the heart about Jesus being the Bread of Life. Perhaps he mentions that Jesus gives us every provision, and as He offered His life up for us, we offer our coming day to Him. Bruce asks the Lord to bless the bread offering.

Then we take the cup. I like to use pomegranate juice because it has a bitter taste, as did the cup of suffering our Lord Jesus' body offered on our behalf. As the cup is lifted up, Bruce offers a short prayer about the blood of Jesus that saves, redeems, and heals. He may also ask the Lord for healing in body, soul, or spirit for the guests gathered as we partake of this cup of remembering.

Bless

I've wondered if I should write a chapter on the blessing. Entire books have been written about the power of blessing and our words. I'm reminded of a retreat for the healing of our souls where participants are invited to receive a father's hug. Lines of men and women, young and old, lining up for a father's affirmation. There are so many people who never had their father's blessing. Here at the Shabbat table, the father blesses the wife and children. A weekly blessing!

The atmosphere in the home changes when blessings are spoken. Consider children hearing their father bless their mother week after week. Marriages are enriched. Hearts are healed and changed. One particular dinner, I hosted 16 couples. For the blessing, I instructed each couple to find a private place and bless one another. It seemed as though the air was sucked out of my home. Tears were shed from both men and women. There was a lingering in this holy moment as words of affirmation, love, encouragement, honor, and value were spoken one to another.

This blessing is not a prayer. You are not praying for the person; you are blessing them. For example, one father said to his son, "John, I saw this week how you told your mother the truth when it would have been as easy to make a story up. I bless your integrity. Your word is your honor. I see God strengthening you for difficult situations. I am so proud of you, John, and I bless your good heart." A blessing calls out how you see God in their character, their goodness, their kindness. Oh, friends, this is a rich time that will leave your children marked forever. I was particularly moved reading of a woman who survived years in a concentration camp. Her testimony of what kept her was the memory of her father laying his hands on her head and blessing her every Sabbath. Think on that!

On two separate occasions, I hosted families with five and six children respectively. Both homes are places of blessing. At one home the father blesses the children at bedtime every night. At the other home the father speaks life into his children and shares what God is showing and saying to him on a regular basis. Although familiar with their father's blessing here at the Shabbat dinner, the children of all ages lean in, waiting expectantly for their turn. What is their father going to say that speaks life, affirms, and blesses each one? The power of those moments cannot be reduced in written words, though they will be written forever on the hearts of the children. There is a Shabbat anointing on this blessing!

In *The Gift of Rest*, Joe Lieberman speaks of his children coming to the table, knowing that no matter how much trouble they got into that week they would receive a father's blessing. Now, even as grown adults, they look to this part of the Sabbath meal as pivotal for their life, week, and relationships.

Enjoy

God wants us to enjoy Him and each other. Sabbath is a celebration! There is a lightness of heart even in the worst of times. There is a joy in fellowship that speaks to the loneliness. There is a laughter that is good medicine for the body, soul, and spirit. Sonia, my Israeli tour guide, told our team that it is not allowed for a Jewish person to be alone on the Sabbath. There are Jewish websites that connect people, college students, and families to others who are opening their home for Sabbath. It's a beautiful thing. There is so much to enjoy about Sabbath—the people, the food, and of course, the presence of God.

Although my example speaks to a traditional family, please know the principles are the same! I have provided for you a template which can be used at any gathering, whether you're single, a college student, a single parent, or just want to have a special night with friends. Many colleagues travel and have resorted to videoconferencing family for a time to worship, pray, bless, and enjoy! What matters is to make this meal special and set apart for the Holy One, Blessed Be He. Not so much the how but always the *Who*!

I reluctantly bring this chapter to an end. My heart's desire is for to you to know that the presence and pleasure of God rests on this special celebration. May your heart be stirred to worship, pray, bless, and enjoy your Sabbath. Now, go plan your celebration!

Every day they continued
to meet together in the temple
courts. They broke bread
in their homes and ate together
with glad and sincere hearts.

Acts 2:46 NIV

36

LEAVE IT ALL ON THE FIELD

> One Sabbath Jesus and His disciples were walking through a field of grain.
>
> —Mark 2:23 (VOICE)

Recently, I was presented an opportunity to do something for the Lord—something totally outside my comfort zone. My ultimate response ("Yes, I'll do it") came from a mandate to walk through every door He opens when given an opportunity to talk about prayer. On this occasion, I spoke to a group of women for 40 minutes, and a spontaneous ending rolled off my heart and out of my mouth: "I love you. God bless you on your journey. I'll see you in heaven." As I walked off the platform, this thought came to me: "I left it all on the field."

I later asked the Lord what He was saying. First, the ending salutation of "See you in heaven" was out of nowhere. However, the likelihood of ever seeing again any of the 160 women in attendance that day was highly unlikely. We crossed paths for a destiny-moment and left charged to go about our Father's business and reunite in heaven! It's God's love for each other that fuels us and sends us. Second, the phrase "left it all on the field" was foreign to me. Google helped. This message, made famous by football legend Coach Vince Lombardi and now echoed by coaches everywhere, refers to giving the task all you've got—talent, heart, character, faith, passion, and courage!

I want to talk to you about your field. What gift, task, prayer assignment, opportunity, or testimony has God built in you? What doors has He opened that no man can close? What does it mean to you to leave it all on the field?

Ruth left it all on the field. She asked her mother-in-law Naomi if she could go glean grain in a field and perhaps find favor (see Ruth 2:2). It was in this field that Ruth caught the attention of Boaz and found his favor. He instructed her, "Do not go to glean in another field ... *Keep* your eyes on the field which they reap" (Ruth 2:8 NASB). When Naomi realized it was Boaz their kinsman, she directed Ruth to anoint herself and go to Boaz at night. When sleep came, Ruth was to uncover his feet and lie down. What an example of living outside your comfort zone! And there's even more. When Boaz awoke and saw Ruth, the young woman made a godly appeal for him to take her under his wing (see Ruth 3:9). Was that a proposal? Bold! Courageous! Brave!

Don't you agree that Ruth left it all on the field? This young Moabite woman positioned herself in God's destiny for her life. She didn't know it at the time, but God knew she was walking into history. Not only did Ruth become the great-grandmother of King David, but she also took her rightful place in the lineage of our King of kings, our Lord Jesus Christ.

The Lord asks us to give our all and not to limit ourselves by our personal expectations, intimidations, insecurities, or past failures. Rather, we are to *leave it all on the field*. This is no time for "Here I am. Send someone else." No! We have entered a period God has prepared for the Church, and an emerging prayer movement has risen. Our ears are tuned to the covenant promises of God, the growing awareness of the time and season we're living in, and the at-stake destinies of ourselves, families, churches, and nation. Leave it all on the field. Don't hold back, shrink back, or turn back! It's time to advance as a praying Church!

Pray those bold, strong, and courageous prayers that are in you. Pray those prayers that scare you. Pray those prayers that bring the very presence of God into difficult situations and circumstances. Pray those prayers only God can answer. Pray with earnestness and desperation. Come, Lord Jesus!

A dear friend, well into her 35-year career as a flight attendant for a major airline, found herself working an especially difficult trip. An atmosphere of persecution, mocking, harassment, and intimidation drove her to tears. She literally put her head into a buffet oven (it was turned off and cool), and through praying tears she asked God, "Why? Why?" He immediately answered, "Thank you for being here for Me." She returned purposed. Her witness of peace, faith, love, and kindness brought the presence of God into an otherwise contentious situation. She left it all on the field for the glory of God.

After nearly four decades of military and commercial aviation, my retired husband responded to a God-burden for Ukrainian orphans. Carrying the love of Jesus, Bruce made nine trips to orphanages in Ukraine. He initiated relationships with local stores and was able to purchase new items for the children. He traveled with suitcases full of clothes, coats, shoes, and supplies to precious children who needed a hug from "Papa" as much as anything else. In addition, he was able to play a part in assisting a couple in adopting three children. Pure joy! He left it all on the field for the glory of God.

Each one of us has a field. We must be willing to ask the difficult questions. Who? What? Where? When? Why? How long? We all have a sphere of influence, a bloom-where-we're-planted assignment. Look around your world. Use God's heart, eyes, and ears to work your field. So often we long for last year's field when God has clearly moved us forward. Or we are looking at and longing for (and dare I say, coveting) someone else's field. Sometimes we find ourselves tripping over the "when." Graduate? Move? Marry? Make a career change? We think, *Oh, I will do that when my circumstances change*. But God wants us to cultivate the field where we are presently planted. We can do this. We can bring His presence into every conversation, situation, hurt, concern, sickness, death, grief, loss, etc. We can leave all we have on the field God has planted us in today.

Mark 2:23 tells us, "One Sabbath Jesus and His disciples were walking through a field of grain" (VOICE). Our I AM God wants to walk with us through our field. I imagine Jesus, our Bread of Life, walking through our field, just like Boaz, the kinsman-redeemer. We plant and water. We glean and see a harvest.

Well, that just makes me want to shout, "Hallelujah!" Honestly, such joy rises in my spirit when I consider Luke 10:2: "The harvest is plentiful, but the workers are few. Ask the Lord of the harvest, therefore, to send out workers into his harvest field" (NIV). We stand among the workers. I'm so proud of you. I'm so blessed by God's people responding to a worldwide emerging prayer movement. We will not say, "It's still four months until harvest" but instead will respond to the Savior's voice: "I tell you, open your eyes and look at the fields! They are ripe for harvest" (John 4:35 NIV). The time is now!

My friend Cindy is a general in prayer and intercession and in leading nations to "leave it all on the field." She once told me, "Never give your assignment to someone else." Oh, I needed to hear that! There are so many times when we disqualify ourselves or compare ourselves to others and come up short. In my "field" as the pastor of prayer and intercession, there were times when the battle raged, and the task was overwhelming and way above my spiritual pay grade (or so I thought). I wanted to give my field to someone more qualified! I'm so grateful my friend gave me that advice.

Let's make a commitment to the Father, Son, and Holy Spirit to leave it all on the field.

> First responders, leave it all on the field.
> Teachers, leave it all on the field.
> Married couples, leave it all on the field.
> Single adults, leave it all on the field.
> Parents, leave it all on the field.
> Students, leave it all on the field.
> Pastors, leave it all on the field.
> Believers, leave it all on the field.

Lord Jesus, we want to be those disciples who walk through the field with You. As we contend for Your move in our churches and our nation, give us the strength and joy for the task set before us to leave it all on the field. In Jesus' name, Amen.

37

ABOVE MY PAY GRADE

I am someone who likes to read the last chapter of a book first so I know how things will turn out. But in real life, God sometimes—oftentimes—surprises me with an unexpected interruption that would change the last chapter as I perceived it.

Well into our retirement years, the financial carpet was pulled out from under Bruce and me, and we found ourselves moving out of state, away from family, friends, and church ministry. Weeks later, no one was more surprised than I was when I enrolled at Wagner Leadership Institute for a concentrated time of discipleship, training, mentoring, and lots of prophetic words about God's plans for me (all of which sounded grandiose). The school wasn't free, but God had said "I want you to go there," and He directed us to make some financial decisions that made my attendance possible.

While I attended Wagner, I kept asking the Lord what this interrupted season was about. Each time, the Author of my life replied, "I know, and I'll let you know what you need to know when you need to know it." That's it! For two years that was all I got. It was like faith, hope, and love rolled up into our blessed Trinity.

God takes us places we wouldn't choose to go to prepare us for what He planned for us. This life-interruption finally began to make sense when I "happened upon"—much like Ruth "happened upon a field" (see Ruth 2:3)—God's foreordained, pre-planned, and I've-prepared-you-for-this transition. My "happened upon" was an only-God, one in a billion "chance" (divinely planned) meeting in a hall with a pastor at the church we attended before we moved. A casual "How are you?" turned into a God-conversation when this pastor told me he had been praying about someone to come on staff to develop a culture of prayer. This person's assignment would be to equip, mentor, and mobilize prayer.

Just then, God whispered in my ear, "This is that." What?! *This* is what I needed to know, but how can *that* be? *Me?* The idea of being a culture developer was such a foreign concept, but settled in my spirit was Isaiah 30:21—"This *is* the way, walk in it."

Fast forward a few months. I officially began what would develop into a 17-year assignment as the pastor of prayer and intercession at Gateway Church. To suggest I was living and serving outside of my comfort zone would be an understatement. But that's where the Holy Spirit lives, isn't it? He dwells outside our natural abilities and forces us to draw on the strength, wisdom, and guidance of our God. The assignment was way over my pay grade but never above His.

As the church grew and the demands of ministry grew with it, I learned the best way to serve was to decrease so He could increase (see John 3:30). I lived from my prayer chair, listening, pondering, praying, and obeying.

Here are a few of the lessons I learned during my staff tenure. When reading these, please don't filter by the title of "church staff person." We are *all* in full-time ministry. Regardless of where or how we serve, we are commissioned to be light, salt, and disciple-makers. I encourage you to ask the Holy Spirit how these points will serve you as you serve Him.

1. DON'T DISQUALIFY YOURSELF. (HEBREWS 13:20–21)

As I navigated my way through new territory both in the natural and in the spirit, it was easy for me to look at the qualifications, giftings, and abilities of others and ask God why He didn't pick them. I'll admit I was very hard on myself. I was the oldest pastor on staff with absolutely no papers on my wall that would qualify me in the natural. Additionally, I was the only woman given a churchwide ministry to oversee. Yikes! My honest thought was, "Here I am, Lord. Please pick anyone else!"

It took time, but God got through my hard head to my soft heart. He showed me that my gift mix (how He created me to pray, hear Him, and serve Him) was good enough for Him, and it turned out to be God-enough to accomplish what He had entrusted to me. My fears of inadequacy and intimidation turned into humble "Here I am. Use me" confidence and strength.

And between God and me, we had the most fun knowing and watching what He could do with my little. What an awesome God we serve!

2. DON'T COMPARE YOURSELF TO OTHERS. (GALATIANS 6:4)

I spent too much time wishing, "What if ..."

- What if I could teach like them?
- What if I could learn and process like they do?
- What if I could use notes when I taught?

What a waste of time! It is good to glean and learn from others' fields. A wonderful sage-friend of mine told me, "Learn everything you can from everyone you can." I took that advice to heart, but I also learned it is useless to try to be someone you are not. You must learn to be whom God created you to be. He has gifted *you* and equipped *you* to accomplish what He entrusted *you* to do.

3. DON'T SHRINK BACK. (HEBREWS 10:39)

Saying "yes" to God and His seemingly insurmountable challenges changed my eternity. I am better for the struggles, valleys, and mountains in the spirit. Yes, I have battle wounds. Plenty. There were many battles in which I wish I had been more strategic. They caught me off guard. But I never gave up. Each battle strengthened me for the next.

When Pastor Marcus Brecheen hired me at Gateway Church, I asked him if he thought I could do this. His quick reply was, "Do not shrink back. You are staring at destiny." I am blessed that God surrounded me with colleagues, praying friends, and a husband who believed in me more than I believed in myself. Pastor Thomas Miller saw that I was created to wield David's weapons instead of King Saul's armor; he kept speaking life and pushing me forward into God's unfolding work in and through my life in service. These people saw and understood more of what God was doing in and through me than I did. I pray God surrounds you with people who are for you, believe in your calling and anointing, and continue to encourage you.

4. DO PITCH YOUR TENT AWAY FROM THE BUSYNESS OF LIFE. (EXODUS 33:7–18)

God took this fledging, overwhelmed servant and anchored her in a Tent of Meeting. I learned early on how to stay connected to the presence of God, the voice of God, and the rest of God despite the whirlwinds of activities, deadlines, and demands swirling around me.

I learned how to pitch my tent physically and spiritually when I met with God in my prayer room closet and when I met with others in the courtyard of life. I learned God wanted my "tent" (His presence) to be movable, and I could carry Him into every conversation, classroom, conflict, and challenge. I learned from Pastor Zach Neese, a dear friend, who would physically remove himself from the busyness of work and go sit on a curb to meet with God. I learned that one intentional moment in the Lord's presence was better than a thousand elsewhere, and He would meet with me to refresh, reset, or readjust my heart and soul before sending me back into the battle.

5. DO ACCEPT THE MANTLE GOD'S PLACED ON YOU. (RUTH 3:15)

A mantle represents the call of God and the purpose for which He calls us. Our mantle is placed on us by the Holy Spirit, but we have a choice on whether to wear that mantle and serve under it.

Ruth 3:15 speaks of Boaz filling Ruth's mantle with an overabundance of grain. There's that "presence of God" word again. Grain = Wheat = Bread = Presence of God. God wants to fill our mantles with an abundance of His presence that will go with us and equip us. Our mantles are not unrighteous burdens but rather part of the crowns we will lay down at His feet.

6. DO STAY UNDER THE MIGHTY HAND OF GOD. (1 PETER 5:6)

Service to God may be lonely at times, but we are never alone. Staying positioned under the hand and heart of God as He directs, disciplines, leads, corrects, loves, sings over, and ministers to and through us is the safest place in the world to be.

Living a fasting lifestyle creates a lingering, a leaning in, and a loving awareness of the presence of God. We must walk humbly before our Lord. Pride is the Achilles heel of praying men and women. It is the kryptonite to service in any capacity, anywhere, anytime. We cannot afford to forget Luke 6:20: "Blessed are you who are poor, for yours is the kingdom of God" (NIV).

When we moved away from everything familiar and I enrolled in Wagner Leadership Institute, I had no idea that God was preparing me for my Gateway assignment. Looking back, I now know that the latter would not have been possible without the former. Interrupted seasons can be testing and even trying, but they are important. They are purposeful. My time at Wagner shaped my time at Gateway, and I can't wait to see how my time at Gateway shapes the next part of my journey with Jesus.

38

SABBATH: A CHARGE TO KEEP
The Story Continues

In my #simply70 (my personal hashtag for my 70s decade) Sabbath journal, I inquired of the Lord about my Sabbath journey. I noted absolutely everything, including my desire, holy passion, and pursuit to figure out how this set-apart day from God works in my life. There is holy jealousy deep within me, provoked by His chosen people who celebrate *HaShem* (Hebrew for 'the Name') so intentionally every week. I desire this family, this faith, and this blessing, and I pray it will be grafted not only into my life and the lives of my family but also into the life of the Church. Help us, Lord!

God's response to me was this:

Dear One, rest, rhythm, and pace originated in me. It is who I am. Rest, rhythm, and pace were created, established, and commanded for you from the very beginning of creation. So you ask Me, "What do I think?" My day is a priority, purposed, planned day. It is a prescription written in ink and sealed in My covenant blood. It is a parable, a psalm, a proverb written on your life. It is a good gift given in love. My desire is that you discern and embrace the joy of this body, soul, and spirit gift. We will make Sabbath as a Galatians 5:22–23 day. This is the fruit that will be produced as you walk closely with Me, and we Sabbath together.

Slowly but surely, the Holy Spirit has taught this Mary living in a Martha world how to have a Sabbath that God would call a delight and even holy. It didn't happen overnight. There is, however, an unfolding grace as we are grafted into the heart of Sabbath. There's an intentional, increasing awareness of the presence of God that lingers long after the day is over. There's a growing awakening of "This is the way, walk in it" that becomes a prayer for me personally and for the Church at large.

Sabbath is a lot like the yeast Jesus spoke about: "The Kingdom of Heaven is like the yeast a woman used in making bread. Even though she put only a little yeast in three measures of flour, it permeated every part of the dough" (Matthew 13:33 NLT). When we call out to God about leaning into Sabbath *His* way, accept *His* gift, and sync our hearts with *His* delight, He is sure to answer us! And He will give us great and mighty treasures hidden in the sacred space of this holy, set-apart day.

Like the miniscule speck of yeast that permeates multiple cups of flour and water and causes the dough to rise, God will do the same for us as we learn to remember and keep the Sabbath. I've discovered it is not merely a day to observe; it is a mindset change. And with this mindset change, I cannot think of a single aspect of my life—body, soul, or spirit—that Sabbath has not enriched.

There is no prescription I can give you of "Do this; don't do that." That would be the law. Rather, because Jesus came to complete the law, we receive His grace as we submit our calendars, desires, and hearts to the Holy Spirit. Though not a list of dos and don'ts, there is a measuring rod Scripture gives us: *rest.* Sabbath is a day of no work. It's holy. And as I told you in the "Sabbath: A Commandment" chapter, it's a delightful, extravagantly luxurious, and pampering kind of day. You will have to ask the Holy Spirit what that looks like in your life!

It is never too late to begin observing and remembering the Sabbath in an intentional way. I was awakened to this gift well after my children were out of the house and my grandchildren were grown. I regret not having or knowing about this when they were young. If I could change one thing, it would be adding the value of this day into the heart and soul of our family. But it is never too late, nor is it ever too early. The time to start is now!

Sabbath doesn't just happen; it takes planning. My Sabbaths used to sneak up on me, and as a result, I didn't have the rest or holiness that marks this day. Pre-planning is essential. Here are a few practical suggestions:

1. PICK A DAY.

When I started to observe God's idea of Sabbath, I looked at my calendar. "Well, God, I'm available next Tuesday, but the following week I can't get together until Friday." No more, though. I recall God saying, "Six days of work, one off. Consecutively!" Pick a day—an intentional day. That day will anchor your week. Like the Jewish mindset of Sabbath, the days leading up to it are days to observe (prepare, plan, and anticipate), and the days following are days to remember, reflect, and enjoy the memories. There is a longing and a lingering attached to your Sabbath.

2. PICK A MEAL.

In the "Sabbath: A Celebration" chapter, we took a close look at the Shabbat meal. Let that chapter help you pick a meal that will have a this-is-special feeling attached to it. Pastor A. J. Swoboda, author of *Subversive Sabbath*,[21] writes how he and his wife selected Saturday morning with a traditional pancake brunch as their Sabbath meal. Their hope and intention are that when their six children are all grown up and they hear the word "Sabbath" or smell pancakes, they will have an innate response to the blessings that came to their lives through this holy day.

3. PICK A BLESSING.

Keep in mind that this set-apart, special day is for rest and is to be holy. Rest is more than a nap (although a nap is a great idea). Holy means set apart for God. With that in mind, pick a blessing for yourself (if you're single) or your family that brings rest and is holy. This could be an activity centered around prayer, worship, journaling, or enjoying a family activity together. Or you can pick a blessing for someone else. Share a meal, write a note, bring a gift … the list of ways to bless others is practically endless!

---

21. A.J. Swoboda, *Subversive Sabbath: The Surprising Power of Rest in a Nonstop World* (Grand Rapids, MI: Brazos Press, 2018).

One particular Acts 2:42 Challah-Day, I hosted my church's campus pastors at my house. The group just so happened to include 15 men and two women. The night before I asked the Lord, "You want me to teach 15 men how to measure flour?" And He quickly responded, "Minimize—don't marginalize." There is such an anointing on the message. God's heart for Sabbath speaks directly to each person in such a profound way. I may have pre-measured my ingredients that day to minimize the ins and outs of baking, but I did not marginalize the message. There is so much of God in the preparation, the planning, the anticipation, and the expectation around this holy day that it is palpable.

During the time for questions, a pastor who is a husband and father asked, "Where do we start?" It can be overwhelming at first. It can be very disruptive to life as usual. But you could hear the longing in these pastors to create a place of rest in their homes and to say to their families, "Yes, I work, but today there is nothing more important than the Lord and you." There is value in coming alongside your spouse to create an atmosphere for worship, prayer, blessings, and enjoyment. So I answered the pastor, "On Friday morning, get up and go buy your wife a flowers, candles, and a pair of candlesticks. Pick up some take-out food. When you get home, say to your wife, 'Honey, I don't know what God wants this day to look like for our family, but I want us to figure it out together.'"

God has charged each of us to observe the Sabbath. It is our charge to keep. So be bold and take that first step. The grace given to us by Jesus, the Lord of the Sabbath, will equip and enable us to live a life where the gift, blessing, and anointing of Sabbath will directly impact and influence our lives for the remaining six days of the week. And if that's not enough, the overflow blessing will impact and influence the world of believers and non-believers in which we live.

Expect God to meet with you. Expect God to inspire you. Expect God to give you rest in your body, soul, and spirit. Expect the atmosphere in your home to be changed. Expect the blessing that is for today and watch it become a legacy for future generations.

39

WELL DONE, DONE WELL

There is danger in changing lanes when you're driving on a highway, and there is danger in changing lanes serving the Lord. Timing is important to us. Timing is important to God. We all need to do our part to accomplish the assignment God has given us. Most importantly, you want your service to be pleasing to the Lord when one assignment finishes and another begins. That can be a physical transition (job, move, marital status change, parenthood, widowhood, empty nester) or a spiritual one (prayer assignment for one reason or season, for person, place, or circumstance). Some transitions we choose, and some are chosen for us. These lane changes need God's timing. And His perspective! Often the way you leave one place determines how you thrive in the next.

Serving the Lord in every part of our life leaves us with an innate God-desire to hear, "Well done." Thus was the case recently as I faced a major life change—retirement. I thought, *Lord, I want to hear Your "Well done, good and faithful servant."* I needed to hear His perspective, heart, and thoughts on what was about to be my past season.

"Well *done*, good and faithful servant" (Matthew 25:21) is often used at memorials and celebrations of life to reference a life well lived. Of course, I desire that ultimate laying-my-crown-at-His feet affirmation when I see God face to face. But what about the here and now?

I searched the Scriptures for "well done" and found a nugget in Proverbs 31:29, except these two words were positioned differently. They carried a key to what God was saying to me in this time of transition. "Many daughters have **done well**" (bold added). That's turned around! I knew this Scripture was talking about my interior life—the spirit in how I served. It was so much more about the *being* a servant of the Lord versus the *doing* His service. I determined I would rather hear the Lord say to me, "Many daughters have **done** nobly, *and* **well** [with the strength of character that is steadfast in goodness], But you excel them all" (AMP, bold added).

Yes, Lord, may Your character be reflected in everything that we do and in however we serve, with prayer and intercession. As we come boldly and confidently into Your throne room, may our character be such a reflection of You that it brings You great pleasure, and ultimately brings us a "Done well and well done."

God confirmed this as I searched the Scriptures regarding finishing well. There is something so special about finishing what you've started. Although the work may not be finished, there is something about knowing that your part is complete. I came across John 17:4: "I have glorified You on the earth. I have **finished** the work which You have given Me to **do**" (bold added). I thought, *How could Jesus say that in John 17 when it's not until John 19:30 He declares, "It is finished!"?*

The answer is simple: the word *finished* in John 17:4 has a different meaning than the same word in John 19:30. In John

17:4, the work Jesus has done was finished. That means His part was carried through to completion—He accomplished what He needed to accomplish to establish His kingdom work here on earth. In John 19:30, when Jesus declares from the cross, "It is finished!" He means that He has carried out the command to defeat Satan once and for all. It is a complete finish of the work Satan began in the garden. At the cross Jesus finished what nobody else could do; only He could complete that command.

John 17:4 refers to the work we were called to do. Our assignment—our part—is finished. But not God's part. No one says it better than Paul in Philippians 1:6:

> I am convinced *and* confident of this very thing, that He who has begun a good work in you will [continue to] perfect *and* complete it until the day of Christ Jesus [the time of His return] (AMP).

As I prepared to transition from my full-time ministry staff assignment to the new plans God has for me outside the walls of the local church, I paused to reflect. I had an all too familiar sense of the weightiness of the assignment. Can you relate? There is a weightiness and joy for the task God has given us. What we do and who we are matters. The spiritual battle is real. God plants, equips, and anoints us to push back the powers of darkness and make a way for the light and glory of God.

Considering the scope of the work, the warfare, the work yet to be done, I said to the Lord, "Did I let you down?" He responded, "No, because you never let go. Now let's go! Mission accomplished."

Our Father will always be faithful to give us His perspective. It makes me think of the report cards schools gave back in the way-way-way long time ago. On the right side would be a list of academic subjects: reading, writing, and arithmetic. On the left side would be character grading: words like effort, conduct, preparedness, courtesy, respect, obedience, and attention. My parents always looked at the left side before they did the right side. Regardless of my academic grade, it was who I was (done well) that carried more weight and applause that what I did (well done.) It seems my earthly parents were reflecting my heavenly Father's desire for who we are to always impact what we do.

40

BECOMING BREAD

Dear friends, here we are at the end of this book—my love offering to the Lord and to you. It's been a great joy welcoming you into my prayer room and kitchen. We've spent time talking, pondering, and processing what bread means to us and how it is reflected in our life of prayer. In the beginning and the end, it's all about Jesus, the Bread of Life, and becoming, living, praying, loving, and serving like He did—His life in and through us.

We are enriched bread. As we follow and partake of His example, teachings, character, and the whole of who He is, we are becoming more like Jesus. As we mature in our relationship with God and grow our prayer life, we are becoming more like Jesus. Becoming bread is cultivating His presence, cooperating with His presence, and carrying His presence with us wherever we go. We become that life of prayer that strengthens others, contends for the will of God, and carries His compassion, mercy, goodness, and faithfulness.

Jesus tells us to remember His ultimate redemptive sacrifice—His giving His life for us—as we take communion. "Do this in remembrance of Me" (Luke 22:19). In these final pages, allow me to take you on a journey through some of Jesus' final days on earth before He ascended to heaven. He was broken for us so that we might be made whole and be released to fulfill His

Great Commission. And if you're able, let's take communion and partake of His bread (body) and wine (blood) together.

Let us go to Gethsemane. Today we're going to go into the garden from where the deepest groans that sent shock waves through heaven and earth came. Where the first drops of covenant blood were shed for you and me. Where the ultimate prayer of "Not my will, but Yours, be done" (Luke 22:42) brought forth God's before-creation plan for you and me!

I've been to Gethsemane in early spring when the ground is lifeless and brown. It reminded me of the wilderness, the desert, and death. The only signs of life and indications of hope were the red poppies populating the ground. Each one looked like a drop of blood. Such holy, surrendered ground. Such brokenness. Such beauty. Jesus shows us His redemptive power in this holy place. We become bread as we learn to live a surrendered life even and especially in our wilderness, our desert, and our brokenness.

Let us go to Golgotha. There on a hill, the great exchange took place—Jesus' life for our lives. There the greatest intercession and mediation for you and me took place.

- Mercy met judgment.
- Righteousness met sin.
- Light met darkness.
- Humility met pride.
- Love met hate.
- Life met death.
- A cursed One on a tree met the curse that originated from a tree.[22]

---

22. Dutch Sheets, *Intercessory Prayer: How God Can Use Your Prayers to Move Heaven and Earth* (Bloomington, MN: Bethany House Publishers, 1996), Kindle edition.

I've been to Golgotha, that city on a hill. Outside the city walls, away from the maddening and mocking crowds, there was the ultimate tent of meeting where Jesus joined the Father and Holy Spirit. Jesus' body was broken and blessed. The most profound moving visual I've ever seen of the moment when Jesus took His last breath was the movie *The Passion*. The moment when Jesus declared, "It is finished," heaven opened, and a tear from our Father fell from heaven to earth, dropping at the foot of the cross where you and I are today. I wonder if that tear is what caused the earth to quake. Here our Bread of Life was broken, and Father God blessed it so we can become more like Him.

Let us go to the Sea of Galilee. Jesus has risen from the dead. The apostles are defaulting to what they know best—fishing. What is in my hand? What was I created to do? What do I know to do? Where is my provision? And then a familiar Friend's voice asks, "Children, have you any food?" (John 21:5). Jesus then gives instruction on where to cast their net. Recognizing Jesus as their Messiah, their Lord, the disciples rush to join Him. Jesus invites them to bring what they caught, and they share a last meal by the seashore where Peter walked on water, Jesus calmed the sea, and the fish and loaves were multiplied. I've been to the Sea of Galilee, and on its shores, I have prayed and met with the resurrected Jesus. He loves to break bread, bless it, and feed His sheep. You and me!

Let us take communion. Throughout this chapter there have been opportunities to look at our life of prayer through the lenses of the Holy Spirit and Jesus' broken-blessed life. Let's celebrate all He has done for us and will continue to do as we pursue a life of prayer by taking communion.

Find a piece of bread, break it, and pray with me:

Lord, this broken piece of bread represents the beauty of Your broken life and my broken life coming together right now. I am ever mindful of the cost You paid and of the cost I'm willing to pay to be one in Spirit. My heart is full of gratitude as I lift up this bread and lift up the name of Jesus. May your life be lifted up and Your name represented in my life as I become bread. Amen.

Now take the cup of water (or whatever drink you prefer):

This cup today, Lord, has water in it, and I'm calling on the very first miracle that you performed at the wedding feast. Turn this water into fine wine. I pray my life will be as new wine—the best saved for last. Lord. I take this cup with a heart full of gratitude knowing that Your blood shed for me has the power and the love to make us one. I take this cup gratefully. Amen.

Just as bread, made of the simple ingredients of flour, honey, yeast, and salt, rises with a sweet aroma, so do our lives of prayer as we cultivate the sacred ingredients of His presence, rest, worship, and Word. The apostle Paul wrote, "Live a life filled with love, following the example of Christ. He loved us and offered himself as a sacrifice for us, a pleasing aroma to God" (Ephesians 5:2 NLT). Let the aroma of our lives poured out for Jesus rise!

I'm praying for your beautiful, broken, blessed, becoming bread life of prayer.

You are a sweet aroma.

Mary Jo Pierce

APPENDIX

MARY JO'S HONEY CHALLAH

I fell backwards into the plans of God when I first fumbled through the mixing, kneading, braiding, and baking of my first challah. But the joy of joining my prayers and heart to generations of challah bakers across the world was as satisfying as eating freshly baked bread. What started as a "This should be interesting" turned into one of my greatest acts of worship. The aroma of prayers and bread filled my heart and home. Let it Rise!

INGREDIENTS

- 5 tsp. (or two packages) active dry yeast
- 1 cup warm water (115°F)
- 1/4 cup honey (1 Tbsp. reserved for yeast)
- 1/4 cup sugar
- 5 cups bread flour
- 2 tsp. salt
- 3 eggs slightly beaten, plus 1 egg intended for glaze
- 8 Tbsp. (1 stick) unsalted butter, melted and cooled*
- Honey crystals, poppy seeds, or sesame seeds (optional)
- Prayers

DIRECTIONS:

Step 1: In warm water add the yeast and 1 Tbsp. honey. Stir. Let stand **until foamy**, about 5-10 minutes. Tip: Heat and sweet activate the yeast. If no foam, start again, as yeast could be old, and your bread will not rise.

Step 2: Using a stand mixer with a dough hook on low speed, mix 4 cups of bread flour, 2 tsp. salt, and ¼ cup sugar. Add the wet ingredients (yeast, egg, butter, and remaining honey) to the dry ingredients. Then add the additional 1 cup of bread flour as needed until the dough separates from the side of bowl and climbs the dough hook.†

Step 3: Knead the dough (approximately 100 times or 5-10 minutes) until it is not sticky and forms a silky like ball (add dusted flour as necessary). **Use this time to pray. For the people who will partake of this bread. For Israel and the families as they make their challah and prepare for Shabbat. For whomever and whatever God puts on your heart.** Press the dough down with your finger to see if it bounces back. Form the dough into a ball and lightly gloss the dough with oil. Transfer it to a lightly oiled bowl.‡ Cover the bowl with a kitchen towel and let it rise in a warm area for 1:45-2 hours.

Step 4: Punch down the dough (this removes air bubbles) and place on counter. Use cutter to divide the dough equally into six sections.§ Roll each section into a cord about 12-15 inches long. Braid **two** 3-cord loaves.¶ Place the loaves on an oiled baking sheet, and cover with a kitchen towel. Let the dough rise until the loaves double in size, about 60 minutes.

Step 5: Preheat oven to 350°F. Gently brush the bread with a beaten egg and sprinkle honey crystals, poppy seeds, or sesame seeds (optional toppings). Place bread loaves on lower third of oven for 25 to 35 minutes. Internal temperature should be 200 degrees. **Tip:** If the bread is browning too quickly, tent with aluminum foil.

Let them cool completely on a wire rack (if you can keep from tasting them right away!). ***This recipe is made with love and served with joy.***

Yield: 2 Loaves

*My personal preference is to melt and cool the butter.

†If you don't have a mixer, add the dry and wet ingredients and then knead until the dough is silky smooth. It will take you longer, but it is very doable.

‡Oil the bowl and dough as this will prevent the dough from sticking to the side of the bowl and not rising.

§I use a scale to weigh the cords. This makes for a more uniform braid, but it is not essential.

¶Braid as you would a hair braid. YouTube has excellent demonstrations for all sorts of braids. Have fun!

If you need assistance, my YouTube channel will walk you through this recipe. Just search www.YouTube.com/mjpraying.

LET IT RISE BABKA

This special recipe is adapted from a favorite of mine. A go-to quick and easy recipe that I originally called "You Choose." It is so versatile! You can add sweet or savory fillings, and this makes a gorgeous loaf or round babka or those must-have rolls.

DRY INGREDIENTS:

- 4 ½ cups flour total (divided)
  - 3 cups initial mixing
  - 1 ½ cups after wet ingredients added as needed
- 4 ½ tsp. active dry yeast or 2 packages
- ½ cup sugar
- 1 tsp. salt
- 1–2 Tbsp. orange zest

WET INGREDIENTS:

- 1 ⅓ cup warm milk (approximately 115 degrees)
- 4 Tbsp. vegetable oil
- 2 eggs (whisked with fork)
- 1 Tbsp. orange juice (optional)

OPTIONAL INGREDIENTS:

- Sweet: Fig Jam
- Savory: Pesto Spread

Step 1: Mix 3 cups of flour with other dry ingredients, adding salt last.

Step 2: Mix the wet ingredients together.

Step 3: Mix dry and wet ingredients together in mixer for 2 minutes on high speed. Then switch to low speed and add the additional 1–1½ cup(s) flour as needed. Use bread paddle to mix ingredients until dough is formed into a ball. It will come off the sides of the bowl and travel up the bread paddle.

Step 4: Knead dough 100 times (avoid adding additional flour) until dough is smooth and bounces back with finger indentation. Then place in bowl with oiled sides and cover with towel. Let rise 10 minutes on warm surface.

Step 5: Roll dough into rectangle shape.

- For Sweet: Spread thin layer fig jam over the dough, stopped at the edges.
- For Savory: Spread thin layer of pesto and shredded mozzarella cheese to cover dough.

Take long edge of dough and begin rolling toward you into a tight, long log. Use a bench scraper or sharp knife to cut down the middle of the log. Place dough up so you can see the layers of filling and begin twisting one side over the other (starting in the middle and working to ends). Place dough in baking pan lined with parchment paper or oiled lightly.

Step 6: Cover and place in a warm spot. Let it rise 90 minutes.

Step 7: Brush top of loaf with egg wash.

Step 8: Bake at 350 degrees approximately 30 minutes until bread reaches 200 degrees internal temperature. (If bread browns too fast, put foil on top until finished baking.)

Yield: 1 Extra-Large Loaf or 2 Bread Pan Loaves

Be creative with your fillings.

- poppy seeds (mix with one whipped egg white)
- fig butter with orange zest
- any flavor jam with butter and nuts
- apple spread
- cinnamon, sugar, and pecans
- spinach and feta cheese
- Nutella and nuts
- sauteed apples, cinnamon, and pecans
- Substitute cornmeal for 1 cup of flour and spread honey, chopped green chilies, and Mexican cheese on dough

Be creative with your toppings depending on the filling.

- Sprinkle with cinnamon and sugar before baking.
- turbinado sugar
- sesame seeds
- cream cheese, confectioners' sugar, and dry espresso coffee
- confectioners' sugar and citrus (lemon, orange, or lime)

Be creative with the shape of the loaf.

- Roll twisted loaf into a circle, tucking ends in.
- Cut into roll-sized portions and turn upward to bake.

- If you want delicious rolls without the twist, you can do that too!

If you want to make a single loaf, here are the ingredient measurements:

Dry Ingredients

- 1 ½ cups flour
- ¾ cups flour (added later)
- 2 ¼ tsp. active dry yeast (one package)
- ¼ cup sugar
- ½ tsp. salt

Wet Ingredients

- ⅔ cup warm milk (approximately 115 degrees)
- 2 Tbsp. oil
- 1 egg

ACKNOWLEDGMENTS

Dear friends, "I thank my God in every remembrance of you, always offering every prayer of mine with joy [and with specific requests] for all of you, [thanking God] for your participation *and* partnership [both your comforting fellowship and gracious contributions] in [advancing]" this book, ***Let It Rise: Sacred Ingredients for a Life of Prayer*** (see Philippians 1:3–5 AMP).

The book you are about to read speaks about sacred ingredients necessary for a life of prayer and special ingredients necessary for an especially delicious loaf of bread. But I want to take a moment to acknowledge the sacred-special people who were involved in bringing this book to fruition.

First and foremost, my husband, Bruce Pierce, whom I affectionately call Brucie: You are my most ardent supporter of what God asks of me. You claim your mission on earth is to take care of me, and to that, you do exceedingly, abundantly more than I could ask or pray! You love the Word of God and obeying the voice of God. At 88, you continue to mentor and disciple others. May God richly bless you and honor your legacy. What a blessed wife am I!

Pastor Thomas Miller: Your compass always points to Jesus. There's a chapter in this book titled, "What If?" and I pause to thank God for my "casual conversation" with you about writing a discipling-mentoring book on prayer, spiritual disciplines, and Jesus our Bread of Life! You encouraged me, prayed for me, and believed in me and this message! What if we had never had that conversation? You're the BEST!

Gateway Publishing Team

- *Lawrence Swicegood*: You recognized the emerging prayer movement impacting the Church and the growing need to equip the saints. You invited me to do my part by writing this book. I'm thankful for your decades of caring for the Church, giving people a voice, and making a way for mine.
- *Stacy Burnett*: For over a decade, I've dreamed about working with you on a book. Your love of God, prayer, and words has blessed me beyond words! Thank you for all the wisdom, counsel, and truth during this writing process. You are an anointed listener. Dear typewriter friend, you are a gift that blesses generations and a true kingdom-partner.
- *Jenny Morgan*: My editor-extraordinaire! You are a special one! You are so gifted with grasping the message of this book and making sure my words reflect the same! You are a 1 Peter 3:4 woman—one adorned with "the unfading beauty of a gentle and quiet spirit, which is of great worth in God's sight" (NIV) and mine! Oh, how you anchored this writer and kept me on course! Thank you, Jenny!
- *Katie Smith*: You are new to Gateway Publishing but not new to me. We have worked on many a devotional together. How blessed I am that you became part of this team in time to work on *Let It Rise*. From cover to cover, your intuitive insights and way with words have blessed this labor of love.
- *Kathy Krenzien, Peyton Sepeda, Alexis Hines, and Chasity Walker*: Your dedication and hard work brought *Let It Rise* from a manuscript to a real book! You are each so gifted in

what God has called you to do. I think of each of you as the binding of a book—you hold everything together!

My Grace-Grace *Let It Rise* Prayer Team: You wouldn't let me give up, shrink back, or quit. Your prayers and encouragement picked me up off many a dusty floor and prayed me back to my prayer chair, listening chair, and writing chair! My 911 warfare calls were met with ready prayer and lots of wisdom too! To my dear Terri Brown, Shirley Kimball, Christa Miles, Kelly O'Briant, and Joanna Wiesinger, I'm eternally grateful.

Hali Bell: You are a prayer gift from God. We only met twice—first at a prayer retreat I was teaching and second around a kitchen island as I taught about challah. God put my name and this book on your heart, and you faithfully sent a weekly text asking, "How can I pray for you?" This is a perfect example of a God-ordained prayer partnership, and I am so grateful!

Quin Sherrer: Special thanks to you, my priceless friend, prayer partner, and author of 30-plus books. Your wisdom, coaching, encouragement, and, most of all, prayers helped birth this book. Thank you, Momma Quin!

Dr. Wayne and Bonnie Wilks: Thank you for your godly counsel and insights!

Casey Cook: Thank you, my brother-in-the-Lord, for real-time prayer texts that spoke faith and put wind under my writing sails.

All my friends who understood my endless "No, I have to write!" replies: Thank you for still being my friends!

Endorsers: I so value and respect each of your personal contributions to this emerging prayer movement and the Church. You use your gifts to "leave it all on the field" God has given you. I am so honored and blessed you took the time to read and comment on *Let It Rise*.

Shared Permissions: Many of these chapters tell your stories—your heartaches, your losses, your finding God in the most difficult of times, and your testimonies of a life of prayer, as well as examples of leadership and mentoring. Thank you for letting us glean from your fields.

Theresa and Raynora: My wonderful sisters, you have known me longer than anyone else! You have prayed and believed for me. You worry about me. You take care of me. With two sisters (Roberta and Bernadette) already in heaven, along with our parents (Theophil and Yula Mae Dobski), I can't say how much I treasure you two here on earth.

As always, my greatest desire and prayer in writing is that this book will be a blessing and inspiration to my daughters (**Toni and Traci**), my grandchildren (**Mackenzie, Bethanie, Grant, Samantha, and Cassidy**), and all the generations that will follow. Loving God, following Jesus, being led by the Holy Spirit, and living a life of prayer is my dearest legacy to them.

For each of you,

> I am convinced *and* confident of this very thing, that He who has begun a good work in each of you will [continue to] perfect *and* complete it until the day of Christ Jesus [the time of his return] (Philippians 1:6 AMP).

ABOUT THE AUTHOR

Mary Jo Pierce, author and speaker, resides in Keller, Texas, with her husband of 44 years, Bruce, and their two Maltese puppies, Honor and Glory.

She is a lifelong student of prayer and intercession, and she delights in discovering the presence of God in everyday life as she shares her passion for prayer, intercession, and Sabbath. Mary Jo loves using every tool available to inspire and exhort people in their prayer lives, including teaching, mentoring, writing, photography, social media, and especially, baking bread! She served as the pastor of prayer and intercession at Gateway Church in Dallas-Fort Worth, Texas, for more than 17 years.

Mary Jo's books *Adventures in Prayer: A 40-Day Journey* and *Follow Me: An Unending Conversation with Jesus* have inspired and unlocked the pure joy of living prayer and studying the Scriptures for thousands of people around the world.

For more teachings on prayer and intercession, as well as stories and recipes from her kitchen, connect with Mary Jo on her website (maryjopierce.com) or on social media (maryjo_pierce.)

NOTES

Fall in love with Jesus all over again.

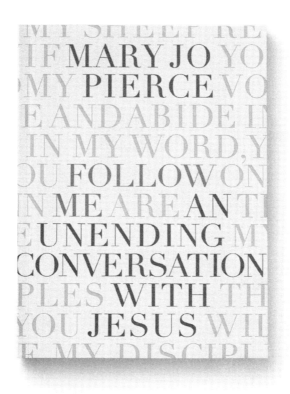

*Jesus wants to talk directly with YOU.
Right now. Wherever you are.
The red-letter words in the book of John
are an invitation to start the conversation.*

ISBN: 9781945529726

Get your copy at GatewayPublishing.com

Praying isn't just talking—
it's also listening, watching, and expecting.

Travel with Mary Jo on her adventures as she finds God in ordinary places. Learn in 40 days what she learned in her first 40 years of walking with God.

ISBN: 9780996566230

Get your copy at GatewayPublishing.com

Also Available in Spanish

Aventuras en la Oración

Cada día de este devocional tiene una historia personal sencilla pero inspiradora. Los elementos del viaje, el carácter y la unción de Mary Jo transformarán tu vida de oración.

ISBN: 9781951227982

Get your copy at GatewayPublishing.com